Competence & Organizational Change

Competence & Organizational Change

A HANDBOOK

Shirley Fletcher

KOGAN PAGE

The National Occupational Standards for Management and TDLB were developed with DfEE funding. This material is Crown copyright and is reproduced under licence from the Controller of Her Majesty's Stationery Office.

First published in 1997

Kogan Page Limited
120 Pentonville Road
London N1 9JN
and
22883 Quicksilver Drive
Stirling, VA 20166, USA

British Library Cataloguing in Publication Data

A CIP record for this book is available from the British Library

ISBN 0 7494 2141 X

Typeset by Northern Phototypesetting Co Ltd, Bolton
Printed and bound in Great Britain by Clays Ltd, St Ives plc

Contents

Acknowledgements

I would like to thank the many people who have contributed ideas during numerous projects over the last few years. My work with a wide range of organizations has led to my having had experience of planning and implementing developments with some very enthusiastic and committed people.

In particular, I would like to thank those people who took time to work on case studies for this book:

DO Eamonn Barclay, Competence Project Coordinator, London Fire and Civil Defence Authority
Alan Clough, Principal Training and Development Consultant
Tim Evans, Remuneration Consultant, ICL
Chris Garner, Organization Development Manager, BUPA
Mark Herring, Operations Manager, Cleaning of Buildings, Sheffield City Council
Gary Ling, Time Manager International
David McCammon, HR Director, Air UK
Alison McLaughlin, TGI Friday's
Linda Nuttall, Training and Development Consultant, Sheffield City Council
Sally Vanson, Group HR Manager, MCL Group
Darren Wood, Cleaning Supervisor/Trainer, Sheffield City Council
Terry Wright, Associate Director, Human Resources, Audit Commission

I have also reproduced a case study on change agent competencies from the UK Learning Organizations Network, originally provided for the second edition of my first book *NVQs, Standards and Competence*. Although this was produced in 1994, it is still relevant in its use and applicability to this topic. The original was produced by Gary Long of TMI following my original contact and work with the Rover Group. The members of the UK Learning Organizations Network are:

Digital Equipment
Lucas
Midland Bank
NHS
Rank Xerox
Rover Group
Royal Mail
Sainsbury's
TMI

My thanks also to the Management Charter Initiative for allowing me to reproduce extracts from the 'hot off the press' revised national management standards. Extracts from national occupational standards are produced under licence from The Stationery Office.

Finally, my thanks to Emma who always manages to produce the final version on time.

Introduction

'Performance Measurement is undergoing something of a transformation'

IRS Management Review, Issue 5, April 1997

The measurement of management of performance is a key topic on the business organization's agenda, with a move away from traditional financially-based measures to a combined financial/quality/people measurement of success and health in a competitive market.

This book draws on recent work with organizations to develop, implement and evaluate integrated performance management and measurement systems. This work has included integration with many of the latest 'trends' in business tools, techniques and methods. Thus, you will find examples of competence frameworks working with:

Balanced scorecard
Cross-functional working
Business process re-engineering
National occupational standards for managers (UK)

Each of these case studies provides a different perspective and context to the use of a competence framework as a component and reference point for change and for the effective management of change.

In the first chapter, I review some of the underlying concepts and models of organizational structure and change. Chapter 2 provides an overview of the concept of competence and its potential for use as a business tool in the competitive company of the millennium.

The third chapter contains case studies and examples of developed and implemented frameworks. Both outcome-based and behaviourally-based competences/ies are discussed, with the proposal that a combination of the best practice from both approaches is the most valuable approach.

The final chapter provides a 'toolkit' for a competence-based approach to Integrated Performance Management.

In the References and Further Reading section I have provided a resource for those who wish to explore ideas, concepts, models and theories further. The materials in this book draw from many disciplines and well-known authors on specialist topics; to deal with all topics in detail would require several volumes.

I trust that readers will use this book both as a stimulus for further research and as a developmental tool.

— 1 —

Organizational Change

1.1 CONCEPTS AND MODELS

One could collect an entire library of publications on the topic of organizational change. This section provides you with an overview and reference point. The References and Further Reading section points you in the direction of more detailed information.

A review of concepts and models of organizational change can assist in identifying a starting point for your own organization. What type of organization do you currently have? What is the driving force for change? What will the changed organization look like?

The role of 'competence' within any organization must be clearly defined. Many existing models of organizations reference this concept, relating it to individual, team, group, division and organization competence. Identifying the current and planned future structure, type and objectives of an organization should always be a starting point for defining and implementing a competence-based system of performance management.

Let us begin by looking at *some* of the key influences and developments in organization structure and management during this century.

1900–1920	Scientific Management (Taylor, 1947)
	Bureaucratic organizations
	Rigid hierarchies and reporting lines (Weber, 1924)
1920s	Decentralization, which continued to be a trend through to the 1960s
	Hawthorne studies (Mayo, 1927–32)

1940s	Concept of the corporation (Drucker,1954)
1950s	Organization principles (Alan Berkely Thomas, 1993)
	Job environment (Herzberg, 1960s)
1960s	Structure follows strategy (Chandler, 1962)
	Theory X and Theory Y (McGregor, 1960)
1970s	Management by objectives (Boston Consulting, 1970s)
	Simple structure organization (Mintzberg, 1989)
1980s	The entrepreneurial organization (Mintzberg, 1989)
	The quality organization (Deming, 1986) (Juran, 1988)
	The shamrock organization (Handy, 1989)
	Enforced change and discontinuity (Peters and Waterman, 1987)
	The art of Japanese management (Pascale and Athos, 1986)
	The post-entrepreneurial organization (Kanter, 1984)
1990s	The learning organization (Senge, 1990)
	Excellence (Waterman, 1994)
	Flatter hierarchies (Drucker, 1954; Handy, 1989)

This list does not, of course, make specific the many theories, tools and techniques which have advocated, in their time, approaches to organizations as 'machines', as 'diversified structures', or as professional, innovative, missionary or knowledge-based structures. We might also add models and techniques such as business process re-engineering, the balanced score card, cross-functional working and ISO 9000 as contributors to change across and within organizations (see References and Further Reading). Most, if not all, of these models, theories and techniques are briefly reviewed in this book, either in the information and planning sections or within the case studies provided by businesses currently managing change with the use of competence frameworks. The text therefore provides an introduction to these models and techniques, with examples of application.

A review of concepts and models – what type of organization are you in?

Perhaps the most radical changes in the structure and management of organizations have taken place since the early 1980s. The bureaucratic model, with strict hierarchies, survived, and is still surviving, but is gradually giving way to the flatter, participative models advocated by such gurus as Tom Peters. The interest in the 1980s in the Japanese style of business management is still prevalent in some sectors of industry.

The following text outlines some of the key components of various concepts, models and theories of organizational structure. There are also checklists for you to consider how your own organization matches up. You may well find that a combination of components from different models appears relevant. If so, consider how this reflects any changes in senior management over the past few years as well as any external influences on the nature and key markets for your business.

Japanese management

Soft 's'	**Hard 's'**
Style	Strategy
Shared, or superordinate goals	Structure
Skills	Systems
Staff	

This organization model defines the 'soft' and 'hard' values of organization management. Consider your own organization – is the focus more on the 'soft' or on the 'hard' values? What do you think a staff survey might indicate in this respect?

These 'soft' and 'hard' values were identified as key differences between Japanese and US organizations by Pascale and Athos (1986) in *The Art of Japanese Management*, based on McKinsey's 'Seven Ss' model (see Table 1.1). Japanese companies, it was proposed, were far better at combining strategy, structure and systems with the 'soft' values; whereas US companies were focused on the 'hard' values. It was suggested that the Japanese were able to compete more effectively in the international market because of this broader combination of values which were operated throughout the organization. The idea of 'competence' both in terms of individuals and the organization is inherent in the 'soft s' components.

Table 1.1 Definition of the seven Ss (adapted from Pascale and Athos (1981) *The Art of Japanese Management*)

Strategy	Plan or course of action leading to the allocation of a firm's scarce resources over time, to reach identified goals
Structure	Characterization of the organization chart (ie, functional, decentralized, etc)
Systems	Proceduralized reports and routinized processes such as meeting formats
Staff	'Demographic' descriptions of important personnel categories within the firm (ie, engineers, entrepreneurs, MBAs, etc). 'Staff' is not meant in line-staff terms
Style	Characterization of how key managers behave in achieving the organization's goals; also the cultural style of the organization
Skills	Distinctive capabilities of key personnel or the firm as a whole
Superordinate goals	The significant meanings or guiding concepts that an organization imbues in its members

The magic number seven

Peter Drucker (1954) recommends that seven layers is the maximum necessary for any organization – although Tom Peters (1988) insists that, today, five layers would be more appropriate.

Seven seems to be something of a magic number in organizational theory. William Ouchi (1981), also proposed that there were seven major distinguishing characteristics of successful US companies. He referred to these as 'Theory Z'; this built on Douglas McGregor's (1960) 'Theory X and Theory Y'. In brief, McGregor proposed that 'Man is a wanting animal – as soon as one of his needs is satisfied, another appears in its place'. As management trainees are well aware, his 'Theory X' employee dislikes work, shuns responsibility and needs to be coerced and directed with a 'carrot and stick' to perform satisfactorily. His 'Theory Y' person welcomes work and responsibility and believes that 'commitment to objectives is a function of the rewards associated with their achievement'.

Ouchi took this work further to identify 'Theory Z' which suggested that Japanese 'clan' and family values such as trust, involvement, loyalty and cooperation were reflected in the business operations of the most successful US companies. Rosabeth Moss Kanter (1989) also suggested that there are seven skills and sensibilities for managers to cultivate (see section 1.2), and Peter Schwartz (1991) suggests 'Seven steps to developing scenarios'.

These examples serve to illustrate where the role of competence becomes important within an organization. The concept of the importance of skills, of staff, of shared goals, of trust, loyalty and involvement, all suggest that a focus on people performance, and on the link of that people performance to corporate goals, is an essential component of the business of the future. How we define these competences and how we use them must be led by the type of organization we are aiming to create.

Let us consider some further examples.

The bureaucratic organization

Max Weber proposed that the bureaucratic organization was the most effective system of management and administration. Weber suggested that in a bureaucratic approach, the basis of authority lies with the office rather than the office holder. Use the checklist in Table 1.2 to see how many of the principles of bureaucracy apply to your organization.

Table 1.2 The bureaucratic organization *Theory of Social and Economic Organisation* (1924) (adapted from Extract, *Organisational Theory* ed D S Pugh (1990))

A continuous organization of official functions, bound by rules	
A specified sphere of competence. This involves: a) a sphere of obligations to perform functions which has been marked off as part of a systematic division of labour b) the provision of the incumbent with the necessary authority to carry out these functions c) the necessary means of compulsion are clearly defined and their use is subject to definite conditions.	
The organization of offices follows the principle of hierarchy; each lower office is under the control and supervision of a higher one.	
There is a right of appeal and of statement of grievances from the lower to the higher offices.	
The rules which regulate the conduct of an office may be technical rules or norms. In both cases, if their application is to be fully rational, specialized training is necessary.	
Only the person who has demonstrated an adequate technical training is qualified to be a member of the administrative staff of such an organized group, and hence only such persons are eligible for appointment to official positions.	
The administrative staff of a rational corporate group consists of 'officials', whether the organization be devoted to political, religious, economic – in particular, capitalistic – or other ends.	
It is a matter of principle that the members of the administrative staff should be completely separated from the ownership of the means of production or administration.	

There is a complete absence of appropriation of his official position by the incumbent. Where 'rights' to an office exist,... they serve the purpose... of securing the purely objective and independent character of the conduct of the office so that it is oriented only to the relevant norms.	
Administrative acts, decisions and rules are formulated and recorded in writing, even in cases where oral discussion is the rule or is even mandatory.	
The combination of written documents and a continuous organization of official functions constitutes the 'office' which is the central focus of all types of corporate action.	

Max Weber's view of organizations was driven by a perception of the structure of authority – what we nowadays call a 'dinosaur!' If we were to define competences for a bureaucratic organization, what values might underpin them? Control and authority are key components of this model. We might therefore find that the management style and organization values led to a framework which focused very much on the management role, with procedural and reporting channels taking prime focus in the measures of successful performance.

The shamrock organization – Charles Handy

In his book *The Age of Unreason* Handy (1990) refers to the 'shamrock organization'. Once again, try the checklist – see Table 1.3. Does any of this seem familiar? Certainly many organizations today are 'downsizing', or 'restructuring' in one way or another. The use of external contracted suppliers appears to be increasing with 'competitive tendering' in the public sector and 'contracting out' in the private sector.

Table 1.3 The shamrock organization adapted from text in Handy, C. (1990) *The Age of Unreason*

The first leaf: Qualified professionals, technicians and managers who own the organization's knowledge which distinguishes that organization from its competitors. These people are rewarded with high salaries, and fringe benefits ('hoops of gold') in return for hard work, long hours, commitment and flexibility	
The second leaf: Non-essential work is contracted out to people who make a speciality of it and who should, in theory, be able to do it better at a lower cost	
The third leaf: The flexible labour force – part-time and temporary workers who are the fastest-growing part of the employment scene. Convenience for the management has been weighed against economy and economy has won	
The temptation is to exploit the monopoly power of the organization, to pay minimal fees for maximum output	
The challenge is to resist that temptation and to pay good fees for good work There is no residual loyalty to be relied on, no promise of security in return for obedient labour	
Contracts are more explicit; good work must, in the long run, receive good rewards, or it will cease to be good work	

Consider what competences in this type of organization might look like. We might rightly expect that they would look somewhat different from those in a bureaucratic organization. What would the emphasis be? How would the different values reflect in the defined framework? Do you think that the emphasis would be on management competences? Or would there be a broader view of competences for a wider range of employees?

The entrepreneurial organization – Mintzberg

This is what Mintzberg referred to as a 'simple structure' organization. Try the checklist in Table 1.4.

Table 1.4 The entrepreneurial organization (summarized from Mintzberg (1979) *The Structuring of Organisations*)

Little or no staff	
Loose division of labour	
Small managerial hierarchy	
Little activity formalized	
Minimal use of planning procedures	
Minimal use of training routines	
Power focused with chief executive, who exercises it personally	
Formal controls are discouraged as a threat to authority	
Strong pockets of expertise are discouraged	
Chief executive's ideology/vision imposed	

This model seems, at first glance, to be one which is doomed to long-term failure. However, there are many organizations which have been led by a charismatic and respected chief executive (the entrepreneur) and which develop and change to become very successful businesses.

Consider what the competences for this type of organization would look like. There are some similarities with the bureaucratic organization – control, authority, lines of reporting. However, there is, in this model, a lack of formalized procedures – how might this affect the competence framework?

Now let us contrast this with the post-entrepreneurial corporation.

The post entrepreneurial corporation – Kanter

In her book *When Giants Learn to Dance*, Rosabeth Moss Kanter (1989) outlines the following characteristics. Try the checklist in Table 1.5.

Tablee 1.5 The post-entrepreneurial organization (summarized from Kanter (1989) *When Giants Learn to Dance*)

A leaner organization with fewer extraneous staff	
Focused on doing only those things in which it has competence	
More responsibilities are delegated to the business units	
More services are provided by outside suppliers	
Fewer layers of management mean a flatter hierarchy	
The 'vertical' dimension of the company is less important	
The 'horizontal' dimension is key to communication through collaboration	

Kanter suggests that:

> 'the post-entrepreneurial corporation represents a triumph of process over structure. That is, relationships and communication and the flexibility to temporarily combine resources are more important that the "formal" channels and reporting relationships represented on an organizational chart… The post-entrepreneurial organization is created by a three-part mix: by the context set at the top, the values and goals emanating from top management; by the channels, forums, programmes and relationships designed in the middle to support those values and goals; and by the project ideas bubbling up from below – ideas for new ventures or technological innovations or better ways to serve customers.'

Here we have a model in which an organization focuses only in those areas in which it has competence. How might the organization decide where its real competence lies? How is this measured? Would we need a competence framework which identified competences at all levels – individual, team and organization? How would the value system influence what the competence framework looked like? How would the competence framework be used, for what purposes, by whom? Does the focus on 'horizontal' communication influence the style, type, content or format of the competence framework needed?

The learning organization – Senge

'The learning organization' has become a popular term, if rather overused. Try the checklist in Table 1.6.

Table 1.6 The learning organization (summarized from Senge (1990) *The Fifth Discipline*)

The focus is on work as 'learningful'	
It is not acceptable to 'figure it out from the top' and have everyone else follow the orders of the grand strategist	
Effort is made to tap people's commitment and capacity to learn at *all* levels of the organization	
Senior managers have a 'stewardship' role for the organization	
Managers are 'researchers and designers'	
Managers understand the organization as a system and the internal and external forces driving change	
Managers design the learning processes to enable understanding of trends and forces	
Senior managers design the organization's learning processes	

Senge suggests that:

> 'there has never been a greater need for mastering team learning in organizations... Whether they are management teams or product development teams of cross-functional task forces, teams, "people who need one another to act"... are becoming the key learning unit in organizations... Individual learning, at some level, is irrelevant for organizational learning. Individuals learn all the time and yet there is no organizational learning. But if teams learn, they become a microcosm for learning throughout the organization. Insights gained are put into action. Skills developed can propagate to other individuals and to other teams.'

The current interest in cross-functional working reflects this view. The role of competence-based frameworks as a planning, structuring and performance management tool is becoming of increasing importance in relation to this perspective of organization development.

The competences defined for this type of organization would need, again, to reflect the value system and management style. The uses of a competence framework in this context might also be more extensively focused on the integration of learning (acquisition of skill and knowledge) and work (application of skill and knowledge).

Let's try yet another comparison.

The survivalist organization – John Harvey-Jones

Try the checklist in Table 1.7.

Table 1.7 The survivalist organization (summarized from John Harvey-Jones (1993) *Managing to Survive*)

Organization should always be a function of the task you wish to achieve	
Every individual in a business should have one person who is responsible for advising, coaching, rewarding and developing them	
The boss is no longer the supervisor responsible for overseeing the detail of work, but is the coach, back up, mentor and friend	
There is no unique and single solution which can be applied to every company	
Each organizational layer should achieve some identifiable added value	
Establishing organizational layers should be approached top down	
An organization is more than the sum of its individual parts	
The wise board looks for the 'unofficial organization' and for those people who feature largely in it	
One of the aims of organizational change is to remove the impediments which the unofficial organization has sought to get around	

This model challenges much company practice. I am sure we can all think of organizations in which people are constantly saying, 'If only we could change this (procedure/process/requirement)', or those in which people change them anyway in order to get the work done.

The competences required in this type of organization will include an openness to change and to reviewing self-imposed constraints and limitations. The 'unofficial organization' is the one which focuses on getting the work done with the minimum of procedural bureaucracy. The senior management role is to identify and tap this unofficial energy source.

Summary

In this section, we have reviewed a number of concepts, theories and models of organization structure. This has incorporated different value systems, management styles, cultures, objectives and perceptions of people management. I hope that this has served to illustrate that models for structuring or changing organizations cannot be considered in isolation from all these other components – how people are motivated, involved, recognized, rewarded and valued all influence the success or otherwise of a change programme.

For each idea we have reviewed, I have also tried to stimulate thought about both the concept and the role of competence frameworks. The definition and use of competences within an organization must also be led by the values and culture of the organization itself.

To establish the broadest approach to reviewing your own organization, you might also like to consider the following categorization of organization structures from Mintzberg (1989) and reproduced in a very useful reference book by Carol Kennedy (1994):

- Simple or entrepreneurial – a small hierarchy with the power focused on the chief executive, often the founder.
- Machine – central bureaucracy, formal procedures, sharp divisions of labour, a large number of routine operations.
- Divisionalized – market-based divisions loosely held together under a central HQ and appearing to be self-standing.
- Professional – bureaucratic yet decentralized and dependent on the skills of its operating professionals.
- Innovative – sometimes called an 'adhocracy', flexible, organic, solves problems directly on behalf of its clients, eg advertising agency, consultancy.

Here is a classification of organization culture from Handy (1976):

- **The power culture**, ruled by one individual's whim and impulse (usually the founding entrepreneur).

- **The role culture**, sometimes derided as bureaucratic because its strength rests on functions, job descriptions and definitions of authority.
- **The task culture**, mainly project-oriented and dependent on individual expertise working in teams.
- **The person culture**, where the organization 'exists only to serve and assist the individuals within it'.

1.2 MANAGING ORGANIZATIONAL CHANGE

The nature of change

As outlined in the previous section, the nature and pace of change have been unprecedented in the 1980s and 1990s. The increase in concepts, theories and models in this period has been almost exponential.

The main features of recent change might be summarized as follows:

- de-layering to flatter structures
- change to multiple reporting relationships
- jobs designed to grow
- increase in job flexibility
- increase in organizational flexibility
- increasing recognition of project and teamwork
- increased use of technology
- fast development of technology
- focus on roles rather than jobs
- need for clear, measurable and flexible standards of performance at all levels

Several models of change and of change management are used. This section reviews some of those models. The use of models in practice is outlined in the various case studies included in Chapter 3.

The Hay seven lever model of integrated organization change

This model (Hay/McBer, 1992) proposed a number of components for integrated change, led by 'strategic objectives' and focusing on 'results':

- leadership
- values and culture
- reward and recognition
- results
- work processes and business systems
- organization, team and job design
- management processes and systems.

This model focuses on 'realizing strategy through people' and proposes the use of competence frameworks within an integrated change programme.

A practical model for organizational change

Gerard Egan (1988) proposed a practical model with three steps:

1. The assessment of the current scenario.
2. The creation of the preferred scenario.
3. Designing a plan that moves the system from the current to the preferred scenario.

Egan suggested that these three stages are essentially cognitive in nature and therefore their ultimate justification is action that produces valued outcomes or results.

Egan's model (which he calls 'Model B') requires a 'learning organization' culture (see section 2.1). As he states,

> 'The best organizations have a culture of learning and problem solving. They know there is no learning without experience and there is no experience without action.'

This view is supported by Peters and Waterman (1987) who state:

> 'the most important and visible outcropping of the action bias in excellent companies is their willingness to try things out, to experiment. ... There is no more important trait among the excellent companies than an action orientation.' (pp. 134, 154)

Egan also proposes his 'Model A', which has four major parts (Egan, 1988):

1. Business dimensions.
2. Organizational dimensions.
3. Management and leadership.
4. Managing the shadow side of the organization.

Business dimensions focus on the establishment of markets and delivery of quality products/services. Business dimensions can be strategic or operational.

Organizational dimensions include the structure of the organization, and the deployment/utilization of human resources.

Management and leadership – effectiveness in these dimensions is required to make all the others happen.

Managing the shadow includes rational factors that affect both the business and organizational dimensions of the system such as 'the natural messiness of the organization', individual differences, the internal social and political systems and organization culture.

Egan feels that his Model A is a 'business and organizational effectiveness model' which provides an 'integrative framework for understanding companies'.

Organization principles

Alan Berkely Thomas (1993) published 12 organization principles which set out the basis for planning effective organization structure. These were originally produced in *Company Organization Charts*, reproduced in *Controversies in Management* by Thomas (1993).

1. There must be clear lines of authority running from the top to the bottom of the organization.
2. No one in the organization should report to more than one line supervisor. Everyone in the organization should know to whom he reports and who reports to him.
3. The responsibility and authority of each supervisor should be clearly defined in writing.
4. Responsibility should always be coupled with corresponding authority.
5. The responsibility of higher authority for the acts of its subordinates is absolute.
6. Authority should be delegated as far down the line as possible.
7. The number of levels of authority should be kept to a minimum.
8. The work of every person in the organization should be confined as far as possible to the performance of a single leading function.
9. Whenever possible, line functions should be separated from staff functions, and adequate emphasis should be placed on important staff activities.
10. There is a limit to the number of positions that can be coordinated by a single executive.
11. The organization should be flexible, so that it can be adjusted to changing conditions.
12. The organization should be kept as simple as possible.

There seem to be some contradictions in these principles, bearing in mind the other models of organizations and of organizational change we are considering. The authority-focus seems to support a view of the 'bureaucratic organization' (see page 7), while principles of simplicity and flexibility suggest more of an ad-hocracy (see page 16).

The proposal that 'the work of every person... should be confined... to the performance of a single leading function' may also be in conflict with current trends to provide 'jobs that grow' and 'learning organizations' – and yet the requirement for the organization to be 'flexible so that it can be adjusted to changing conditions' appears to be fully in line with many current trends.

Similarly, the proposed separation of 'line functions' from 'staff functions', with 'absolute authority' for line managers, appears to present a bureaucratic, chimney stack approach to company organization and to change management which will not equate well with the current move towards cross-functional working.

The role of competence, or skill, or knowledge is not explicit in this model, nor is the need for adequate staff training, support and reward. This lack of 'people focus' is inherent in many early models where the emphasis was on the organization as (almost) an entity in its own right.

Issues for creating a change culture

The management of change cannot, in itself, be divorced from general management theories. The management style within any organization will directly influence the success of change programmes. Management style is influenced by the underlying values of an organization. It is important, therefore, to match style, culture and values to the objectives and process of change.

You might like to try the checklist in Table 1.8 to identify the most prevalent management style, culture and values in your own organization. The checklist provides an overview of various management theories this century. Consider each in terms of:

1. Which, do you feel, is the most prevalent style in your organization?
2. How does this style influence actions for change?
3. How do the underpinning values manifest themselves?
4. Does this style focus on systems?
5. Does this style focus on control and authority?
6. Does this style focus on people?

Table 1.8 Summary of management trends

Taylor, FW (1911)	*Scientific Management* This approach expounds that maximum efficiency is obtained by breaking down tasks into each component movement, so finding the best, and most efficient way of doing each. This was the forerunner of 'work study', or 'time and motion'. In Taylor's model, the relationship between manager and employees is one of master-servant or parent-child.
Mayo, E (1927–32)	*Hawthorne studies* Perhaps one of the most quoted approaches in respect of people management is Elton Mayo's studies at the Hawthorne Works of Western Electric in Chicago. His findings showed that productivity of workers improved when working conditions were discussed between employees and management – whether or not the conditions were actually improved. His work contributed much to motivational theory. His work (1949) concluded that the difference was the result of feeling part of a team and led to the new idea that workers should be considered to be part of a social organism rather than individual cogs in a large wheel.
McGregor D (1930s)	*Theory X and Theory Y* This theory suggested two different styles of management, based on the underlying assumptions of employee motivation. Theory X requires a 'carrot and stick' model of motivation; Theory Y places problems of human resources in the lap of management; – people will exercise self-direction and self-control in the achievement of organizational objectives, if they are committed to those objectives. Theory Y suggests that authority and control are not appropriate for all purposes and under all circumstances.
Herzberg, F (1960s)	*Job enrichment* Herzberg differentiated between motivational and hygiene factors, the latter being such things as salary and working conditions. In his later work (1968) he suggested that 'in attempting to enrich an employee's

	job, management often succeed in reducing the man's personal contribution, rather than giving him an opportunity for growth in his accustomed job'. He called this 'horizontal loading', which, he suggested, merely enlarges the meaninglessness of the job.
Maslow, A (1960s)	*Hierarchy of needs* Maslow proposed that there is a series of needs to be satisfied for all individuals. As each need is satisfied, the satisfaction itself ceases to be important. The implications for management are an awareness of these needs and action to satisfy them.
Jaques, E (1950s)	*Clarity of roles* While Maslow, Herzberg and McGregor led the field in management and motivational theory during the 1960s and 1970s, research undertaken in London at the Tavistock Institute was gaining interest. Elliot Jaques (1976) proposed that the key for management of people was to have clearly defined and *agreed* roles and responsibilities. He suggested that lack of clear boundaries caused confusion which led to frustration, insecurity and a need to avoid accountability.
Drucker, P F (1954)	*Management practice* Drucker has written on virtually every aspect of organizational management and change. In his *Practice of Management* (1954) he says that the function which distinguishes the managers above all others is an educational one. The manager's unique contribution should be 'to give others vision and the ability to perform.' He also proposed 'management by objectives', 'risk-taking decisions', 'strategic thinking' and 'building an integrated team'.
Boston Consulting Group (1970s)	*Management by objectives* Terms such as 'learning curve', 'growth share matrix', 'stars', 'dogs', 'cash-cows', 'question-marks' and the 'Boston Box' will be familiar to users of this approach. Centred again in the 'scientific management' school, the use of 'decision trees' was prevalent, focusing mainly on investment strategies. Decision-making strategies within change programmes are often led by this approach.

Pascale and Athos (1980s)	*Japanese management* Use of the 'Seven S' framework (see page 6) as a performance measurement tool and for comparison between US and Japanese management styles. Pascale felt that early managerial theory was significant for what it left out – for example, total absence of attention to building a corporate team, or to the recruitment and selection of staff, or to training or socialization within the working teams. He suggested that 'field infantry' value should be acknowledged.
Kanter, R (1980s)	*Change management* Kanter's views focus on the flatter hierarchy, the post-entrepreneurial organization (see page 12), and flexibility of an organization to respond to change. She feels that the first step in change mastery is 'understanding how individuals can exert leverage in an organization'. She refers to 'corporate entrepreneurs' who test limits and create new possibilities by directing innovation. She also refers to 'business athletes' who 'know how to compete in a way that enhances rather than undercuts cooperation'. Integrative teamwork is an important component in this approach, as is developing a broader understanding of 'what happens at different levels of the organization' (Kanter, 1984).
Peters and Waterman (1982)	*Search for excellence* In this joint publication, Peters and Waterman (1987) suggest that 'leadership is patient, usually boring coalition building'. The key of this approach, however, is built on the 'Seven S' (see Pascale and Athos) model. In companies which operate with 'superordinate goals and strong cultures' they found that 'people way down the line know what they are supposed to do in most situations because the handful of guiding values is crystal clear'. Another key component of the excellent company is that 'their systems reinforce degrees of winning rather than degrees of losing… targets and quotas are set to allow that to happen'.

Peters, T (1990s)	*Thriving on Chaos* (1988); *Liberation Management* (1992) In *Thriving on Chaos*, Peters suggests that the most successful organizations are the impatient ones who will 'reorganize on a dime'. Organizations adopting this approach will follow the guide that 'if you are not reorganizing, pretty substantially, once every six to twelve months, you're probably out of step with the times'. In *Liberation Management* Peters stresses the need for more rapid and flexible management responses to the demands of the marketplace with a focus on capturing and retaining the loyalty of customers – going beyond 'satisfied customers' to 'committed customers'.
Waterman (1990s)	*Adhocracy* (1990) In his book *The Renewal Factor* (1987), Waterman says that 'one of the most difficult challenges in management is developing a sense of value and vision'. He also gives 14 guidelines for strengthening team work. In his later book on *The Frontiers of Excellence* (1994) he suggests that a well run total quality programme can be of benefit to middle managers and employees as well as to customers.
Harvey-Jones, J (1990s)	*Managing To Survive* (1993) Harvey Jones feels that the most important personal skill in this decade is that of managing radical change. His view is that no one actually 'manages' change, they 'release and guide it'. He also states that organizations do not change until the people in those organizations have – and people do not change their ideas and values quickly.
Handy C (1990s)	*Understanding Organisations* (1976) Handy's 1976 book outlined differences between a 'power culture', a 'role culture', a 'task culture' and a 'person culture' in organizations (see page 16). His later books, including *Gods of Management*, *The Age of Unreason* and *The Empty Raincoat* have expounded his ideas. He proposed the model of the 'shamrock organization' (see page 10).

I would not claim to have included all the key players in this field in the above synopsis. I hope, however, that consideration of the different views, some building on others, has helped you to think about the starting point for change in your organization, by considering what type and style of organization you have at present. A more detailed and extensive review of the work of various 'gurus' can be found in Kennedy (1994).

Getting the spirit of change into an organization

Chester Barnard (1938) proposed that:

> 'Organizations are a system of co-operative activities – and their co-ordination requires something intangible and personal that is largely a matter of relationships.'

In 1954, Peter Drucker proposed five areas in which practices are required 'to ensure the right spirit throughout management organization':

1. There must be high performance requirements; no condoning of poor or mediocre performance; and rewards must be based on performance.
2. Each management job must be a rewarding job in itself rather than just a step on the promotion ladder.
3. There must be a rational and just promotion system.
4. Management needs a 'charter' spelling out clearly who has the power to make 'life and death' decisions affecting a manager; and there should be some way for a manager to appeal to a higher court.
5. In its appointments, management must demonstrate that it realises that integrity is the one absolute requirement of a manager, the one quality that he has to bring with him and cannot be expected to acquire later on.

Returning to the magic number seven (see page 6), Rosabeth Moss Kanter (1989) also suggests that there are seven skills and sensibilities that managers need to cultivate in order to become 'true business athletes':

- learn to operate without the might of the hierarchy behind you
- know how to compete in a way that enhances rather than undercuts cooperation

- operate with the highest ethical standards
- have a dose of humility
- develop a process focus
- be multifaceted and ambidextrous
- gain satisfaction from results.

Competence and business excellence

The major shift in change management in recent years has been towards team building, strategic thinking and people focus. Various re-engineering tools have been tried, with mixed success, perhaps working best when the overall, strategic view is taken to include process, systems, knowledge and people, rather than focusing on any one – or missing out any one – of these.

The strategic use of competence frameworks of various kinds (close encounters of the competence type!) has proved to be a valuable approach worldwide. When linked with the introduction of a quality programme (see Fletcher, 1993), the well-used term 'people are our most important asset' can be made to come alive in an organization.

People's value to an organization needs to be measured, for that to happen; measures must be produced and people must be given clear indications of what those measures are, how to achieve them and how they will know when they have achieved them. The measures defined must link *directly* to business performance measures, or no one will see the purpose behind the measurement framework and no one will be motivated to use it.

It is the application of this common-sense approach to organizational change and development that manifests in the use of competences/ies as a common language for business and people systems. The integration with a focus on quality is highlighted in use of the 'Business excellence model' in the Air UK case study (see pages 61) the 'Profit and loss account of competence' in the BUPA case study (page 72) and the 'Competence/change toolkit' (see Chapter 4) (see also Fletcher, 1993).

Summary

In this section I have outlined some different approaches to change management and made the point that any change programme must take account of the starting point of the organization. Although change is constant, it does not happen overnight when people's attitudes, beliefs, values and the expectations of their work roles need to change.

The overview of various management theories has, I hope, stimulated thought and, perhaps, provided a reference point for future planning and research.

1.3 ASSESSING ORGANIZATIONAL CHANGE

A starting point

Logic would suggest that a change programme in any organization must begin with assessment to establish a starting point.

Where are we now?

By establishing key issues for change – and the required components of that change – action can be taken. This action must be continually reviewed and evaluated.

How are we progressing?

Measures of progression must themselves be based on an ultimate goal.

Where do we want to go?

The assessment of change is therefore a continuous process; see Figure 1.1.

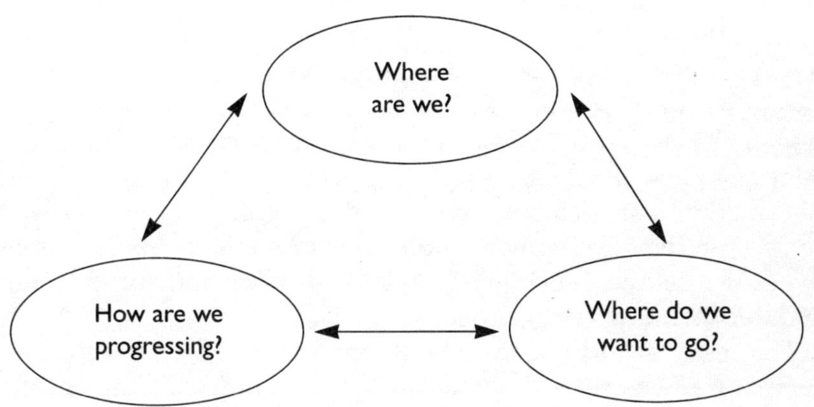

Figure 1.1 Change is a continuous process

This section examines some key issues, implications and models of organization assessment.

Unique or generic rules?

The basis for assessing organizational change must be to compare prior states with later states. To understand the state of an organization, one must compare it with other organizations. To understand the causes of change, potential causal factors and their links to different outcomes must be explored. Kurt Lewin's model (1969) for unfreezing – changing – freezing is one which suggests that the 'before and after' stages have some element of stability.

Challenges to this hypothesis might be made on the grounds that each organization is unique, perhaps due to complexity. For example, Porter and Millar (1979) consider the issue of identity in respect of the structure and processes of living systems. Similarly, if we adopt the view that 'change is constant' it is difficult to reconcile this to supposed stability at any point in an organization's development or operation.

Perhaps, however, we could consider that aiming to understand the generic components of organizations and the measurable aspects of organization behaviour will assist with defining the uniqueness of any individual organization.

Michigan Quality of Work Program

In 1972 the Michigan Quality of Work Program (MQWP) initiated research into the assessment of quality of work life and into the economic performance of work organizations (Seashore, 1983). This research included a number of change projects including those relating to new plant start-ups, compensation, communication and information management. The second component of this research centred on the development and testing of methods for describing the structure and functioning of organizations and for detecting and documenting changes over time.

The research did not include commitment to any specific conceptual framework or theoretical approach; however, four principal guidelines were used in selecting approaches. In summary, these constituted a preference for:

- concepts representing results
- concepts and variables relevant to understanding of such results
- concepts and variables that exploit contemporary theoretical and empirical resources to aid understanding of results, causa-

tion, contingencies and variances
- concepts and variables that allow comparisons among and within organizations.

Consideration was also given to concepts that could be measured in ways that would be perceived as valid by a wide range of observers. The broad mandate was to identify measurable concepts relevant to individuals, groups, sub-units and the organization as a whole.

The programme identified these three basic issues for assessment of organizational change:

- the validity of the comparative method
- the explication of causes
- models of the effectiveness to be employed (Seashore, 1983).

Seashore suggests that assessment of organizational change requires:

- an assessment of considerable scope, cost and intrusion
- a very hospitable research site (which must be developed through preparatory work)
- the collection and synthesis of diverse kinds of data from diverse sources
- the use of longitudinal measures and comparison units.

A global map

A further model for assessing organizational behaviour was presented as a global map by Lawler *et al.* (1983).

They proposed that assessment should be based upon an encompassing theoretical model of organizational behaviour and change and not upon an ad hoc choice of outcome criteria and control variables. They suggested that the use of such a model will focus attention on the 'full array or variables and conditions that might have a role in the understanding of the evaluation outcomes'.

Secondly they felt that an assessment programme should rest upon information obtained in a 'describable and replicable way', so that its nature and quality may be independently judged. A third requirement, in their view, is that the design of the assessment programme should allow for the diminution of plausible but invalid interpretation of the findings.

They proposed a 'global map' to be used for the identification of the key determinants of organizational effectiveness; this is illustrated in Figure 1.2

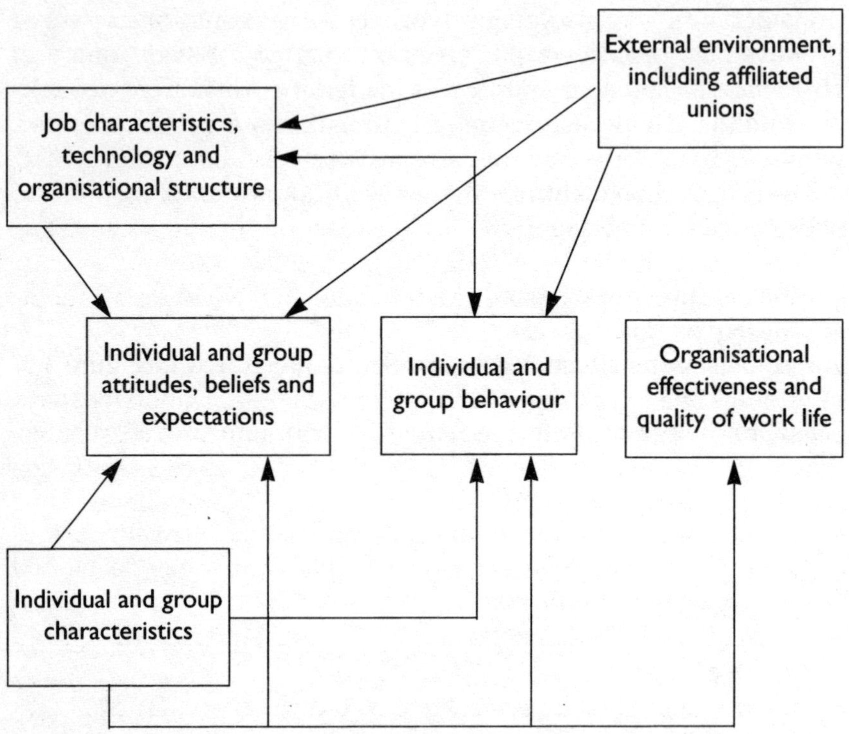

Figure 1.2 Relevant classes of variables in assessment of organizational behaviour (Lawler *et al.*, 1983)

'Prior' causes in this global map model include the attributes of individuals mapped into the organization as well as the attributes of jobs, subsystems and their surrounding organization characteristics.

This model suggests six broad classes of variables for assessment:

1. *Effectiveness outcomes*: may be productive output-rate, quality, cost of production, or cost, timeliness and quality in service organizations.
2. *Individual and group behaviour*: individual effort, problem-solving methods, supervisory teamwork, inter-group conflict, resolution.
3. *Individual and group attitudes and beliefs*: shared beliefs and social norms, membership and job satisfaction.

4. *Job characteristics, technology and organization structure*: the variety, autonomy and significance of jobs and the effect on cooperation; the type and nature of technology used and the servicing provided; the appropriateness of the work flow, the existence of 'buffers', use of professional services and ease of information flow; how the structure influences beliefs and values.
5. *Individual group characteristics*: people with different backgrounds, sexes, races, levels of education, job preferences and abilities; the effect of this mix on an operation, achievement, teamwork, productivity.
6. *External environment*: how the organization 'fits' in its environment, market factors, stability, degree of competition, presence and strength of unions and their relationship with management.

The connections between these factors, as illustrated in Figure 1.3, suggest that there is a seventh component of organizational behaviour for assessment, which is referred to as 'connectedness' ie, an organization is more than a collection of parts; effectiveness is influenced by 'global systemic properties of the organization'.

Taking an holistic approach

This type of model of organization behaviour suggests that assessment of organizational change cannot be undertaken effectively unless an holistic approach is adopted – the system must be considered 'as a whole', with each component interdependent.

Competent organization

Assessment of competence can take many forms and depends on *what* is being assessed.

In my recent work with BUPA (see case study, page 72), 'competence' was defined at several levels; see Figure 1.3.

- *Strategic competences* – otherwise known as organizational or core competences – are measures of the effective organization. For BUPA, these were linked directly to the 'balanced score card', an approach developed by Kaplan and Norton (1996) and currently adopted by companies to provide more specific measures of business performance. Using BUPA's balanced score card as a basis for ultimate measurement and conducting an in-house competency analysis, we defined competencies. These

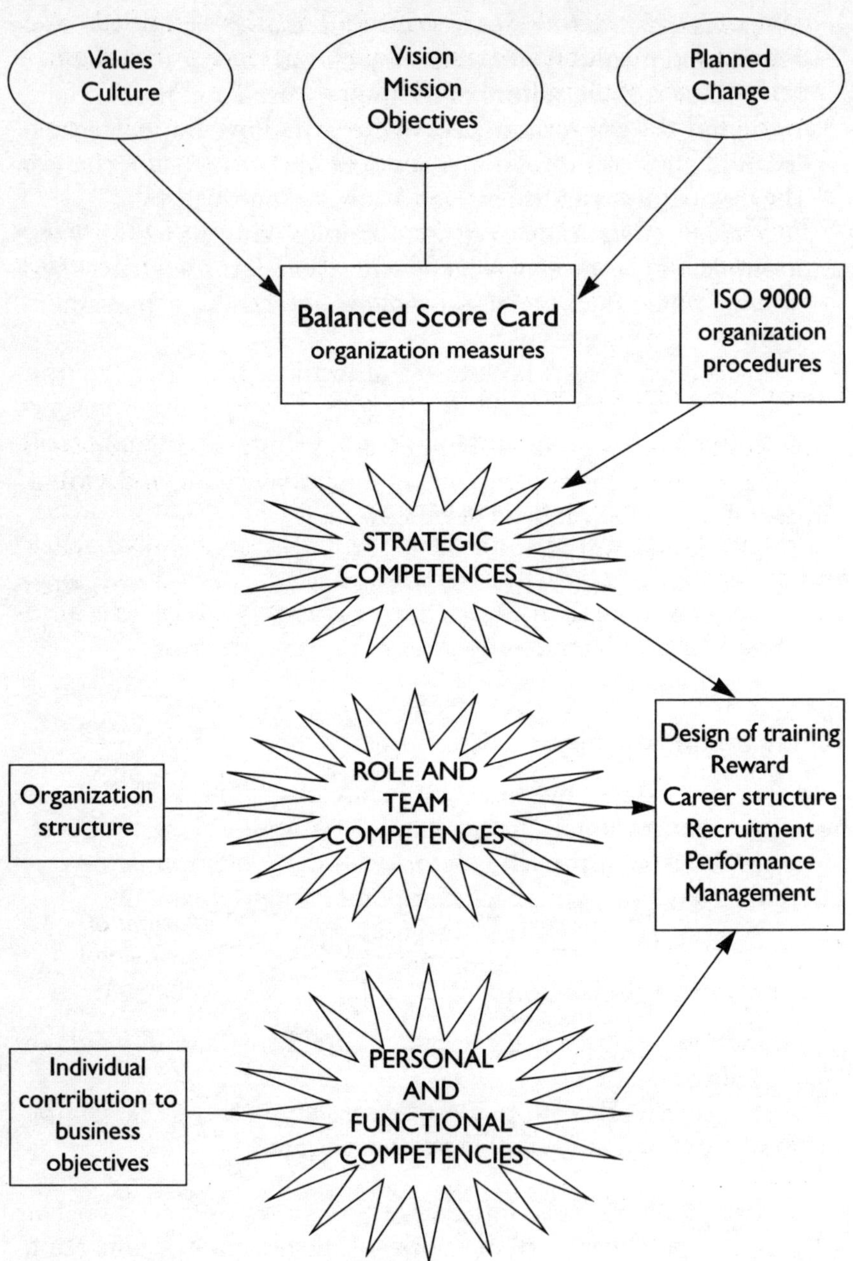

Figure 1.3 Competence: an integrative business tool (see BUPA case study)

competencies included descriptors which identified and defined organizational measures of competence – the *collective* performance of all individuals and groups.

- *Management competences* – these reflect the desired behaviours *and* outcomes for effective management performance and style. The organization's (desired) culture is a key component.
- Functional competencies – *these reflect the competences which underpin functional and cross-functional working, with functions being defined as sales, marketing, administration, etc.*

A profit and loss account of competence

In the BUPA example, assessment of organization effectiveness is undertaken through assessment of competence at individual, group and organization level (see Figure 1.4).

All individual competences are linked to strategic competences, thereby providing individuals with clear indications of how their performance directly contributes to business performance.

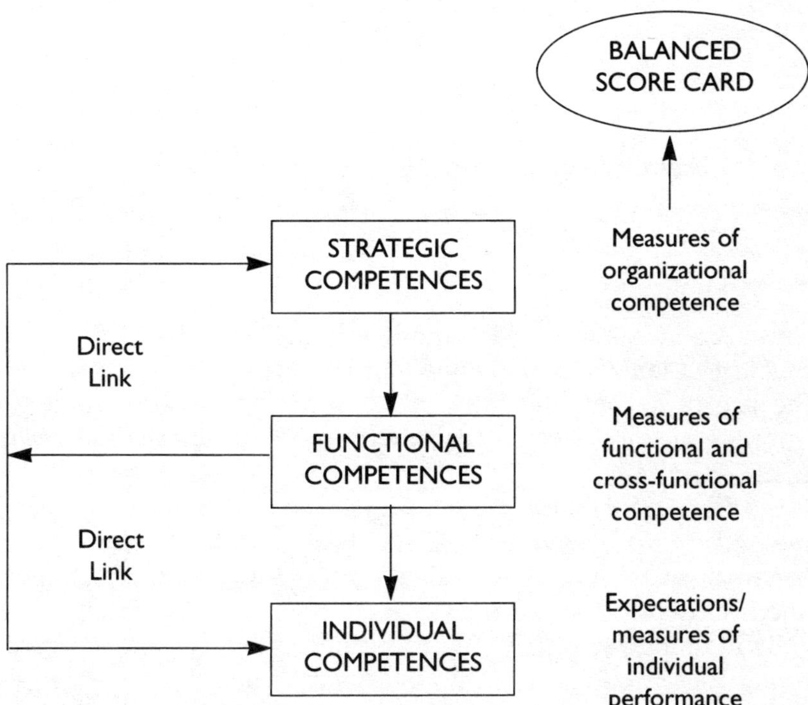

Figure 1.4 The BUPA approach to assessment of organizational competence

The competence framework and the assessment system were computerized, allowing a 'Profit and loss account of competence' to be produced at regular intervals and establishing the basis for a 'paperless' office (see Figure 1.5). Analysis by 'competence' type will be undertaken in order that action to facilitate change is targeted to the right areas.

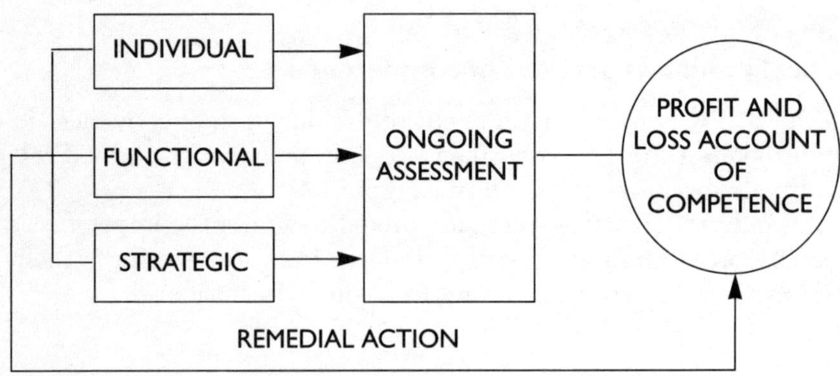

Figure 1.5 BUPA's 'Profit and loss account of competence'

Summary

This section has outlined some key issues and models in assessment of organizational change and has provided one example of the use of a competence framework for progressing change to improve business performance, with measures at all levels being established.

A key point of all the models and issues outlined is that individual and group behaviours, values, beliefs, skills, knowledge and motivation are major components of organizational effectiveness and thus of organizational change.

By defining *expectations* of groups and individuals and incorporating these expectations into everyday planning and action, we can provide a framework for organizational improvement, development and change.

The next chapter deals with 'competence' as a concept and as an operational tool. Defining the concept and agreeing a common interpretation is critical to success of any competence-based project. I therefore suggest that you review the next chapter carefully before moving on to the case study and toolkit sections.

— 2 —

Competence

2.1 INTRODUCTION

This chapter outlines key concepts, issues and factors affecting the development and use of competence frameworks within business organizations. Some of the information contained in this chapter was also included in my book *Quality and Competence* (Fletcher, 1993) and has been adapted for this publication. Different models of competence are explained with examples of their use.

Clarity and common interpretation of the concept and of the intended purpose of a competence framework are critical to the success of a development and implementation programme.

- What does the term 'competence' mean to you?
- Do you usually refer to 'competences' or 'competencies'?
- Does your organization have defined competences(ies) for
  Managers?
  Supervisors?
  All employees?
  The organization as a whole?

Defining competence

Many organizations have management competencies of one type or another. These are often defined by 'examining individual management jobs separately and specifying the personal qualities required' (Handy *et al.*, 1988). Handy found that most UK organizations (61 per cent) adopted this approach, with personality and job experience being perceived as the most important factors.

In his book *Outcomes* (Jessup, 1991), Gilbert Jessup refers to 'competence' in respect of the UK system of National Vocational Qualifications (NVQs), saying that 'a shift has taken place from the determination of competence primarily by those in the education sector (further education and awarding bodies) to those in the industrial sector (employers and employees) through the network of industry bodies'. He refers to perceptions that this will lead to a 'narrow' concept of competence, based upon immediate job requirements and concedes that this has been the case in some industries.

He then goes on to clarify the intended meaning of competence by saying that this term does *not* apply to 'a lowish or minimum level of performance'; rather, it refers to 'the standard required to successfully perform an activity or function... performing to professional or occupational standards'.

The issue of breadth is critical in defining competence. In business, performance in any occupation or profession demands not only successful performance in the technical requirements of a *job* but also in the wider aspects required of a work *role*. These wider aspects will include teamwork, communication, time management and interpersonal skills. In contrast, in the outcomes-based approach adopted in the UK system of vocational qualifications, the 'behavioural competencies' approach is also widely used. This approach focuses on 'looking at the way people behave as a predictor of performance' (Boulter *et al.*, 1992). This focus is the Hay/McBer model or style of behavioural competencies, defined in dimensions and clusters (see page 46). Boulter goes on to say that 'decades of research have proven that past behaviour is the best predictor of future behaviour, so competencies are usually assessed through interviews which probe how the interviewee actually behaved in past work-related events'.

If this is the case, what are the implications for using competencies as the foundation for a change programme? From the above statement one might deduce that behaviour change is 'too difficult' and the answer would therefore be in recruitment of the 'right people', with the 'right attitude'. This certainly helps, *if* the desired competencies are clearly defined and incorporated into a recruitment and selection programme and if assessment tools are designed with the purpose of assessing *potential* rather than performance.

Competent people as change agents

As the previous chapter illustrated, the majority of theories and models of organizational structure, change and assessment have a key component – people. The phrase 'people are our most important asset' is often used, but rarely actioned to its full potential. The greatest change agents are people and yet businesses rarely give these people clear and measurable standards by which to work, improve and understand their own contribution to the success of the business.

Powerful actions for change can be initiated and completed, if we give people the power to do so. This power must come from understanding the importance of individual's roles to business success.

If we first define what we mean by 'competence' and then define clear measures of competence, *linking these directly to business performance*, we can provide each and every employee with the power to improve that business performance. A competence framework then becomes a valuable business tool which drives human resource policy and practice and acts as a 'skeleton' on which the 'flesh' of human resource functions can fit. Issues of training and development, recruitment and recognition can all be developed from one framework.

Similarly, quality initiatives can be incorporated into this framework. All quality measures require *action by people*. A competence framework should include these actions *at every level* – defined clearly in context for each individual to understand not just concepts, but their *application*.

If there is no link between individual performance and business objectives how can real results be measured? How can 'competence gaps' and real training needs be identified?

Understanding competence

This section provides an overview of the two main concepts – behavioural competencies and outcome-based competences.

Your initial work on a competence-based change programme must start with agreement on the nature and purpose of your competence framework (see Fletcher, 1993, 1997c). You may decide that you really need a combination of behavioural and outcome-based definitions for your competence framework. This can be achieved and draws on the best from both approaches. (For further information and examples of this combined approach see the case studies in Chapter 3).

In the UK, national, qualification-driven competence-based systems are based on standards defined by industry. However, this is not the only competence-based approach available.

The confusion which many people experience can involve debates on, for example, competence systems which are

criterion-referenced	vs.	criterion-validated
outcome-based	vs.	behavioural
outcome-related	vs.	input-related
competences	vs.	competencies
competence	vs.	competency

In many cases, the issues of terminology tend to take over and lead to theoretical or academic debates at the expense of real progress.

When considering competence-based assessment systems, the first consideration should always be the needs of the users. Questions such as, 'What do we want to assess?' and, 'Why do we want to assess?' are far more important at the outset. Without answers to these simple questions, any discussion on technical issues will remain in the circular, theoretical realm.

First, a brief review of basics.

Which competence-based system?

The competency-based movement has been in existence for some time. From the 1960s onwards, however, there has been an increasing demand in the business world for greater accountability and more effective means of measuring and managing performance. This has led to research into what makes people effective and what constitutes a competent worker. Consequently, several different models of 'competence' are in use, to meet different needs.

USA – early models in education

It is generally agreed that competency-based education has its roots in teacher education, usually referred to as CBET – competency-based education and training – and that its development was fuelled by the US Office of Education's funding for the development of model training programmes for elementary school teachers. These models included 'the precise specification of competences or behaviours *to be learned* [note the emphasis on 'learning'], the modularization of instruction, evaluation and feedback, personalization and field experience' (Swancheck and Campbell, 1981).

Establishment of these models led to a demand for certification policies which aimed to improve school provision through the reform of teacher education. This became known as PBTE – performance-based teacher education.

As might be expected, the introduction of CBET in the USA caused a strong reaction from the higher education institutions, which perceived this new trend as a threat to their autonomy and academic status. A system of this kind also requires considerable reorganization of resources – an issue which affects the education and training arena at all levels.

The introduction of CBET in the USA was, however, supported by the US Office of Education, which promoted the new trend through the National Consortium of Competency-based Education Centers. This Consortium established a set of 'Criteria for describing and assessing competency-based Programs' (see Table 2.1). The text also refers to criteria for 'instruction', for 'governance and management' and for the 'total programme'. The emphasis is on 'learning' and on 'instruction' rather than on assessment of actual workplace performance. This type of competence specification is most often used as part of a 'competence development programme'. It is essential to be clear, therefore, whether the key purpose of the competences(ies) is *development* or *assessment of performance*.

Difficulties arose in the USA because compliance with all the requirements within these stated 'criteria' meant a complete review and reorganization of the education system.

This early model was focused on teacher training and very much centred in the educational forum. Plans to expand this to the vocational sector were hampered by the misunderstanding that the vocational system had always been competence-based! In fact, the USA system, like that in the UK, was one in which curricula were devised centrally for institution-based education and often placed more emphasis on theory and knowledge than on practical application in the workplace. Federal funding was made available to stimulate the use of competence-based systems in the vocational sector, but the emphasis remained on PBTE.

Table 2.1 Criteria for describing and assessing competency-based programmes (Source: National Consortium of Competence-Based Education Centers - USA)

Competency specifications

1. Competences are based on an analysis of the professional role(s) and/or a theoretical formulation of professional responsibilities.
2. Competency statements describe outcomes expected from the performance of professionally-related functions, or those knowledge, skills and attitudes thought to be essential to the performance of those functions.
3. Competency statements facilitate criterion-referenced assessment.
4. Competences are treated as tentative predictors of professional effectiveness and are subjected to continual validation procedures.
5. Competences are specified and made public prior to instruction.
6. Learners completing the CBET program demonstrate a wide range of competency profiles.

Assessment

13. Competency measures are validly related to competency statements.
14. Competency measures are specific, realistic and sensitive to nuance.
15. Competency measures discriminate on the basis of standards set for competency demonstration.
16. Data provided by competency measures are manageable and useful in decision making.
17. Competency measures and standards are specified and made public prior to instruction.

Guidance on the development and use of competence-based systems of learning and assessment began to proliferate. A further model was proposed by Elam (1971) and has been used extensively to explain competence-based systems in respect of vocational education and training. It provides a useful starting point – but one word of warning: make no assumptions about understanding of the terminology used! One mistake frequently made is that of recognizing the terms and assuming 'we already do that!' The fact that many of these aspects of competence-based provision have been 'tacked-on' to existing curricula does not make the revised product 'competence-based'! Notice again the use of the terms 'progress', 'learning' and 'programmes' in Table 2.2 below.

Table 2.2 Characteristics of competence-based programmes (Source: Elam, 1971)

Essential Elements

1. Competences are role derived, specified in behaviourial terms and made public.

2. Assessment criteria are competency based, specify mastery levels and are made public.

3. Assessment requires performance as prime evidence but takes knowledge into account.

4. Individual student progress rate depends on demonstrated competency.

5. The instructional programme facilitates development and evaluation of specific competences.

Implied Characteristics

1. Individualisation of learning.
2. Feedback to learners.
3. Emphasis on exit rather than admission requirements.
4. Systematic programme.
5. Modularisation.
6. Student and programme accountability.

Related Desirable Characteristics

1. Field setting for learning.
2. Broad base for decision making.
3. Provision of protocol and training materials.
4. Student participation in decision making.
5. Research oriented and regenerative.
6. Career continuous.
7. Role integration.

USA – Hay/McBer models

A second model that is widely used is concerned with the identification of characteristics of superior performers in an occupational role. It is often referred to as the system that relates to 'soft skills' or 'soft competencies'.

The work originates with McLelland at the McBer Corporation and Harvard Business School. Competencies (note the difference in spelling from the UK 'competences') are derived through a form of critical incident analysis, using highly successful or 'excellent' performers as a research group. The resulting 'underlying characteristics' are organized into 'clusters' and have been used in management education and training in the USA and in the UK.

The basic concept of this model differs from that introduced in the UK (see below). The McBer competency system is based on the underlying assumption that 'competence' is defined in terms of the 'characteristics' of individuals. In this respect then, 'competence' is something which is 'held' or 'owned' by the individual and brought to the occupational role. This type of competency is usually produced in the form of descriptors or dimensions and clusters, similar to those in the Air UK Case Study (page 61) and as described in others in Chapter 3.

The UK competency system

In the early 1970s, the New Training Initiative (MSC, 1981) first launched the idea of 'standards of a new kind'. White Papers in 1986 and a review of vocational qualifications in the same year led to the beginning of the standards development programme. The then Manpower Services Commission (MSC) was charged with managing the development of 'occupational standards of performance' for all sectors of all industries.

The review of vocational qualifications in England and Wales also led to the establishment of the National Council for Vocational Qualifications (NCVQ)* which was to take responsibility for the development of criteria for a framework of qualifications based on these new 'employment-led' standards of competence.

A huge development programme began. Industry Lead Bodies were established and charged with project management responsibilities for standards development within their own sectors. The Standards Methodology Unit at the MSC managed a wide range of projects to establish the methodology for the development of standards and associated assessment and certification systems.

The UK standards of occupational competence are different in format and in basic concept from those in the US system (see Figure 2.1). They are also being developed for *all* occupational roles in *all* sectors of industry and commerce. In the UK, competence-based standards reflect the expectations of workplace performance. The establishment of 'personal competences' to supplement these occupationally-related standards has been included in the revised management standards (see Table 2.3).

*NCVQ became the Qualifications and Curriculum Authority (QCA) in 1997.

UNIT TITLE:	**A1 MAINTAIN ACTIVITIES TO MEET REQUIREMENTS**
ELEMENT TITLE:	**A1.1 MAINTAIN WORK ACTIVITIES TO MEET REQUIREMENTS**

PERFORMANCE CRITERIA

You must ensure that

a) you agree **requirements** with **customers** in sufficient detail to allow work to be planned
b) you explain **requirements** to **relevant people** in sufficient detail and at an appropriate level and pace
c) you confirm with **relevant people** their understanding of, and commitment to, meeting **requirements**
d) your monitoring of your team's work takes place at appropriate intervals and complies with your organisation's procedures
e) the work under your control normally meets agreed **requirements**
f) when products, services and processes do not meet agreed **requirements**, you take prompt and effective corrective action
g) records relating to the work under your control are complete, accurate and in line with your organisation's procedures
h) you give opportunities to **relevant people** to make recommendations for improving work activities.

KNOWLEDGE REQUIREMENTS

You need to know and understand

Communication

- how to communicate effectively with team members, colleagues, line managers and people outside your organisation

Customer relations

- the importance of a focus on customer requirements and quality issues, and your role and responsibilities in relation to this
- the differences between internal and external customers
- how to identify customer requirements to a level of detail sufficient for planning work

Involvement and motivation

- how to encourage and enable team members, colleagues and line managers to help to improve efficiency

Monitoring and evaluation

- how to monitor work activities and take corrective action to ensure requirements are being met

Organisational context

- the records which need to be completed and how this should be done

Planning

- the principles of planning work activities, setting objectives and priorities to ensure requirements are met efficiently

EVIDENCE REQUIREMENTS

You must prove that you *maintain work activities to meet requirements* to the National Standard of competence.

To do this, you must provide evidence to convince your assessor that you consistently meet **all** the performance criteria.

Your evidence must be the result of real work activities undertaken by yourself. Evidence from simulated activities is **not** acceptable for this element.

You must show evidence that you agree all the following types of **requirements**

- quality, quantity, delivery, health and safety.

You must show evidence that you agree requirements with **one** of the following types of **customer**

- internal, external.

You must also show that you explain work activities and provide opportunities for making recommendations to **one** of the following types of **relevant people**

- team members, colleagues working at your level, higher-level managers or sponsors, people outside your organisation.

You must, however, convince your assessor that you have the necessary knowledge, understanding and skills to be able to perform competently in respects of **all** types of **customer** and **relevant people** listed above.

Figure 2.1 Example from revised management standards (Source: MCI, 1997, reproduced under licence from The Stationery Office)

Table 2.3 Traditional vs competence-based assessment (qualification-driven systems)

	Traditional (Course-based)	**Competence-based (Workplace)**
Concept	Assessment of learning ability or achievement	Assessment of actual performance in a work role
Foundation	Curricula defined centrally by teaching staff/divisional boards	Explicit standards of required performance defined by industry (UK) or by research using 'excellent' performers (USA)
Assessment requirements	Assessment is an integral part of learning programmes	Assessment is independent of any learning programme
Evidence	Assessment evidence drawn from course assignments/exams	Assessment evidence collected from actual workplace performance supplemented by other methods
	Types of evidence predetermined by course syllabus	Types of evidence governed only by rules for quality of evidence
	Assessment is norm-referenced	Assessment is criterion-referenced (UK), criterion-validated (USA), and individualized

Starting on the right foot

'We are introducing competence-based performance management' is a very broad statement. If your organization is considering this development, and if you are charged with the initial research or with the implementation process, then consider the following before making any definitive decisions:

- Why do we want a competence-based system?
- How do we plan to use it?
- Which competence-based system is needed?
- What are the key differences?
- What are the implications of each?
- Which system would best meet our needs?
- What do we want to assess?
    - organizational competence?
    - occupational competence?
    - management competence?
    - personal competence?
    - generic competence?
    - functional competence?
    - any combination of the above?

If this chapter has raised more questions than it has answered then I have achieved my objective. Use of the term 'competence-based' is becoming more common, but unfortunately use of its full potential is not. For those considering a move in the competence-based direction, I offer the charts in Tables 2.4–2.6 as a basic reference point and the remaining chapters as a practical guide to that journey. This may be of help in finding your way through the confusion. It may also assist you in making decisions regarding the various assessment systems on offer and their relevance to your organization's needs.

Table 2.4 Key differences between the main types of competence-based assessment systems

Criterion-referenced competences	**Criterion-validated competencies**
Standards of performance (competences) developed and agreed by industry (national) or by the organization (company-specific)	Competency clusters developed by research using 'excellent' performers
Assessment of workplace performance	Learning and development of competence/ assessment of behaviours
Competence = expectations of employment	Competence = personal characteristics
Standards outcome-based (criterion-referenced)	Standards output-oriented (criterion-validated)
Standards of occupational competence (actual performance at work)	Educational process (competence development)
Agreed benchmark of competent performance	Specifications of 'superior' performance defined by educational research
Product – hard competences	Product – soft competences

Table 2.5 Checklist for competence-based assessment

If you are considering the introduction of a competence-based assessment system and perhaps seeking advice from an external source, the following may be of assistance as a checklist for use with the proposals presented. Is the proposed system:

- Based on the use of explicit statements of performance?
- Focused on the assessment of *outputs* or *outcomes* of performance?
- Independent of any specified learning programme?
- Based on a requirement in which evidence of performance is collected from observation and questioning of actual performance as the main assessment method?
- One which provides *individualized* assessment?
- One which contains clear guidance to assessors regarding the quality of evidence to be collected?
- One which contains clear guidelines and procedures for quality

Table 2.6 Key questions for planning the design of competence-based assessment

1. What do we want to assess?	a) Technical competence b) Occupational competence c) Behaviours d) Individual performance e) Group/team performance f) Ability to learn g) Learning achievements
2. Why do we want to assess?	a) to measure individual contribution to business objectives b) to measure group/team contribution to business objectives c) to certificate competence to nationally agreed standards d) to confirm competence against company-specific standards e) to identify potential for further development f) to confirm outcomes of learning

—— 3 ——

The Competent Change Organization

3.1 MEASURING PERFORMANCE: AN INTEGRATED APPROACH

Business organizations today continually search for tools, methods, concepts, models or a box of magic tricks to:

- improve competitive edge
- increase profitability
- clarify expectations
- set measurable performance measures
- align individual behaviour and performance with business goals and strategies
- encourage individuals and groups to take responsibility for their own development
- accelerate the development of leaders
- drive continuous innovation and change.

Trends come and go and popular initiatives are to be found in most HR discussions, where items such as total quality management (TQM), business process re-engineering (BPR), balanced score card (BSC) and cross-functional working become an integral part of any discussion. In the midst of these trends, the concept of 'competence' is not new, but has endured. I would suggest, however, that the full potential of competence frameworks has only just been realized, particularly when linked with the tools of new technology.

Most human resource people will recognize the term if not the format and presentation of competences or competencies. When it comes to defining and using them, however, there is great confusion, often due to a biased view or to an isolated perception. Some people believe that *competences* are definitions of skills and knowledge, and that this should be the case, as these are the only components of individual performance that can be developed and assessed. Others believe that behaviour is a more important part of competent performance and that attitudes, traits and motives form the *competencies* which people bring to a role.

The debate between competence and excellence has also raised its head in both camps, the argument here being that competitive organizations need *excellent*, not simply *competent*, performers.

I would like to propose that the debates between outcome/behaviour and competence/excellence are irrelevant and time-wasting in the context of business organizations. If all organizations aim for competence then competence becomes a benchmark. If some aim for competence and others aim for excellence, does this really make the 'excellence' companies more successful than the competent ones? Does it really matter what we call the standards we define? What happens when 'excellence' becomes the norm? Will we find other descriptors – superlative, super-duper, apex, summit or just plain brilliant?

I find that organizations can spend far too much time word-chasing and too little time achieving a common understanding of goals and objectives. When it comes to competence and competence frameworks, all organizations use them, in various ways, for one overall purpose: to help improve *performance* at all levels.

So, let's talk about competence frameworks as part of an *integrated performance management system.*

Integrated performance management

Here we go with another phrase – 'Define your terms' I hear you say! Okay. What do I mean by performance management? I mean managing, controlling, supporting and continuously improving the success of any business. I mean work performance linked to business performance at every level and establishing the systems and processes to support assessment, review and evaluation.

An *integrated* performance management system is one that approaches the organization as a whole. Inherent within this approach is that the organization, as a functioning entity, is comprised of component parts – but the sum of the whole is greater than that of its individual components. This is because of the added dimension of interaction between all components.

If this interaction is to be managed and empowered effectively, there must be a common framework and toolkit as a reference point for all people within the organization. Figure 3.1 illustrates how London Fire and Civil Defence Authority is approaching an integrated performance management system.

This model links individual performance to organization plans and ultimately to organization objectives. It also uses a competence framework to restructure and redefine roles, to structure progression, and as a basis for recruitment and selection as well as training and development.

The competence framework is the 'backbone' of performance management. All human resource functions use the competence framework as a reference point (see Figure 3.2).

Communications and technology assist by providing a basis for communication flow (Figure 3.3). Because assessment takes place at all levels, performance at all levels can be evaluated and plans developed and implemented. Plans at each level are led by strategy (Figure 3.4). Plans and competencies at the highest level must be based on desired and critical business outcomes. This includes the financially measurable outcomes of productivity and profit, and the less tangible culture measures.

A similar model is in operation at Air UK (see page 61). Here, competences are used as a tool for role profiling and form an integral part of performance management. An interesting aspect of this model is its development into a paperless performance management system, where competences are included in a user-friendly network, along with mission, processes, procedures, appraisal and personnel records.

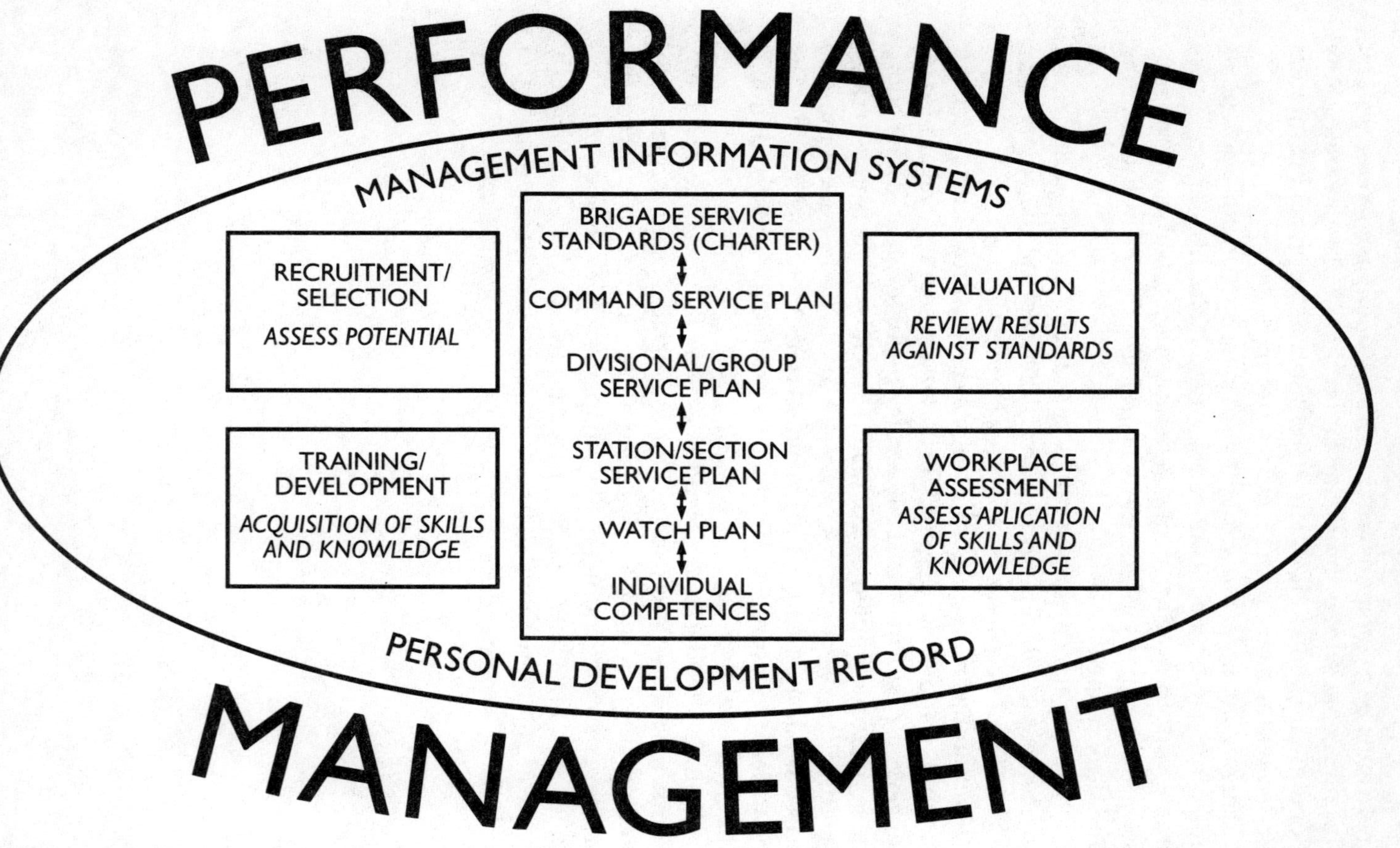

Figure 3.1 Model of integrated performance management (Source: Fletcher Consultancy, 1997. Produced for London Fire and Civil Defence Authority)

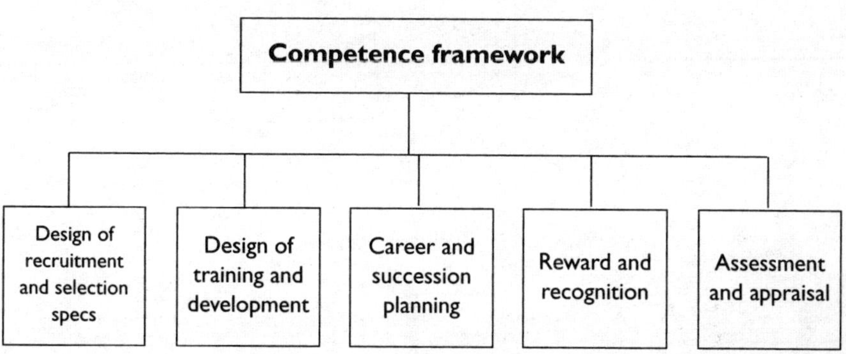

Figure 3.2 An integrated HR function

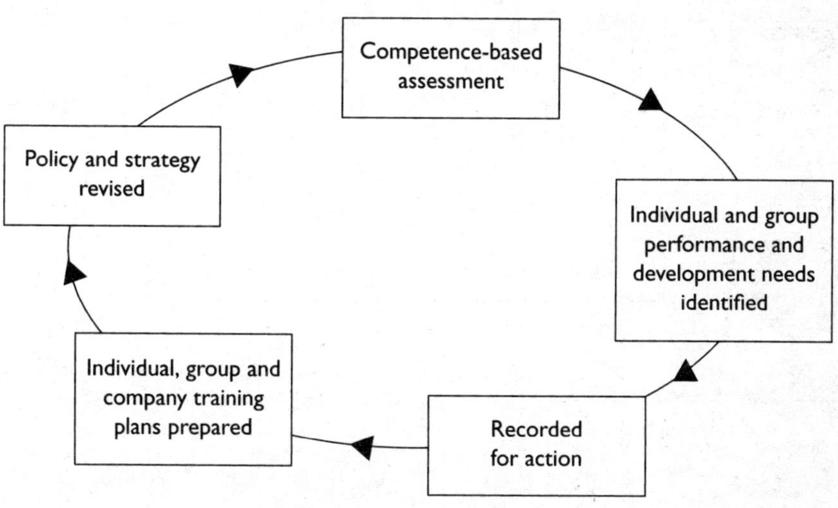

Figure 3.3 Communication flow

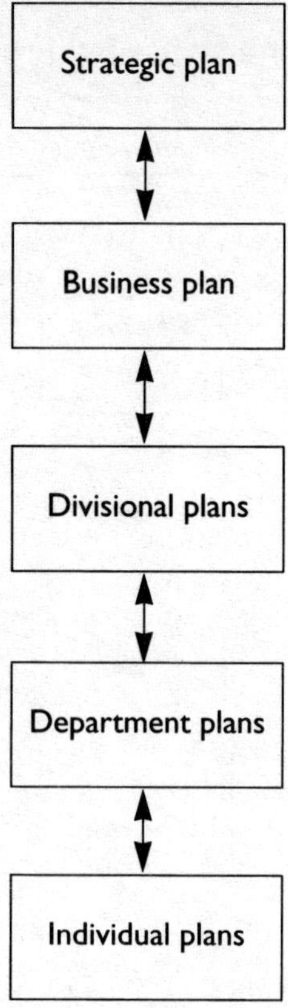

Figure 3.4 The linked planning process

■ CASE STUDY ■

AIR UK

Air UK, recently merged with KLM, has used a competence framework in an integrated way to focus on individual, group and business competencies (note the use of the behaviourally-based 'competencies' term).

Background

The airline industry is extremely competitive and each asset needs to be used productively if a profit is to be earned. Air UK regards its staff as 'its most important asset' and it believes that the way they are managed and motivated has an effect on their productivity and thus company profitability.

With this in mind, one of the elements that it has recently introduced is that of using competencies to assist their integrated management approach (see Figure 3.5). Before explaining how, a brief description of Air UK could be useful.

Air UK employs about 2000 staff, mainly in the UK but with a small number in Europe. The company is owned by KLM Royal Dutch Airlines. Just recently the sales and marketing departments of Air UK and KLM in the UK have merged to present one integrated unit to the market place. The combined sales are in excess of £500m pa – about the same as KLM in their home market of Holland.

Why competencies?

By using competencies, objectivity features in:

- succession planning through competency matching.
- development of staff through identification of their competency requirements
- job family progression through different competency levels.

How competencies are integrated with recruitment, appraisal and induction
During the past six months, Air UK has completely revised its approach to the appraisal of staff. During this time the company has designed an appraisal form applicable to all staff in the airline. To reinforce the importance of this appraisal approach, the Director of Human Resources has personally trained each of Air UK's managers and supervisors on the new approach to appraising staff.

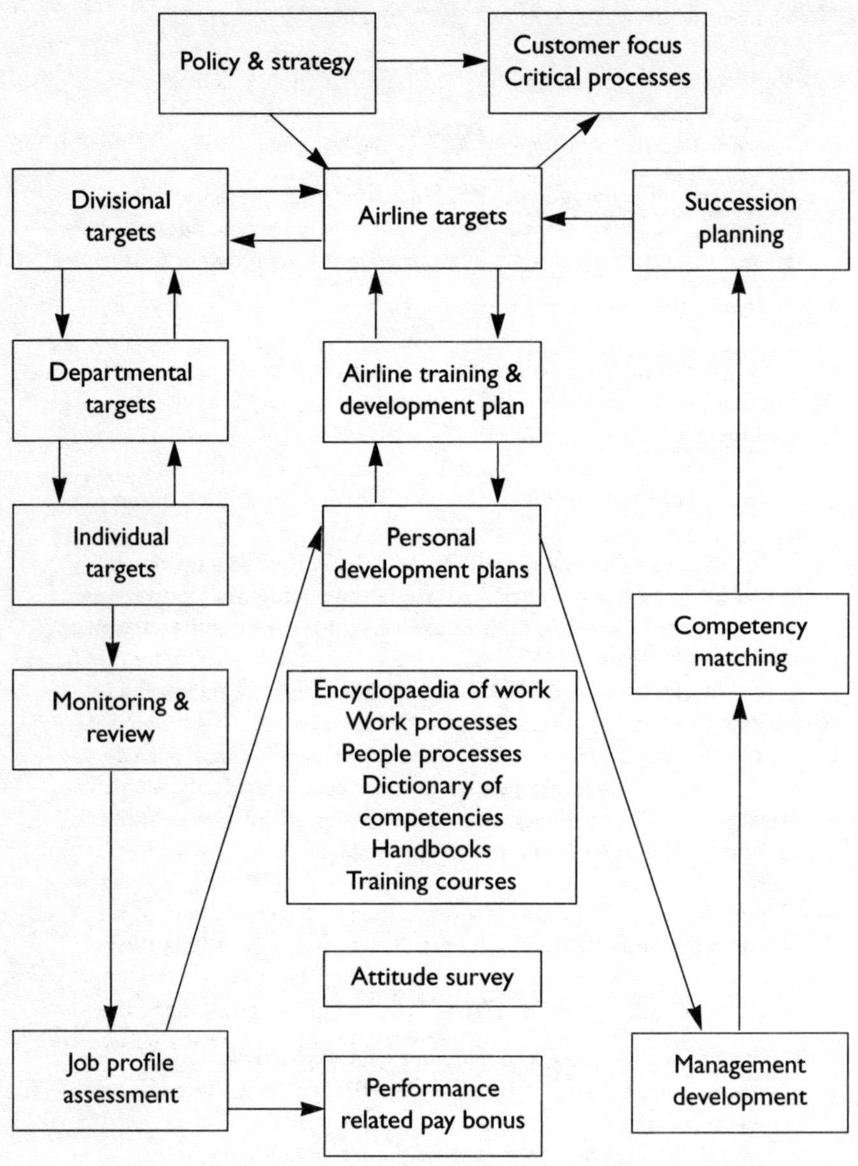

Figure 3.5 Air UK business excellence system (Reproduced with permission of Air UK)

The appraisal exercise seeks to achieve the following objectives:

- to be an important communication opportunity – including structure of work
- to record performance during the past year
- to focus staff on the key targets for the coming year
- to record competency levels
- to note training and development needs
- to note suitability for advancement in the airline
- to record the history of a person in Air UK.

As far as competencies are concerned, all staff are judged on how well they measure up on four key competencies:

1. Customer focus.
2. Professionalism.
3. Achievement drive.
4. Teamwork.

An example of one of these competencies, created with the assistance of Hay management consultants, is given in Figure 3.6. All managers and supervisors have been trained to set a person's appropriate competency level. This means that to be judged as level three, for example, that person must not only possess the qualities in level three but also all those qualities that apply to levels one and two.

Air UK has defined these key competencies as the ones that it wishes to promote throughout the airline and, to reinforce this message, not only are recruitment staff seeking these qualities at the recruitment stage, but this message is further driven home at induction courses where the Director of Human Resources meets all joiners. Part of his talk includes the importance of the staff member demonstrating these competencies if he or she wishes to progress with the airline.

In addition to these company-wide 'core competencies', there are other competencies that have been agreed for senior staff. These will be introduced when the Air UK 'Business excellence system' is introduced later in the year:

1. Strategic thinking.
2. Entrepreneurism.
3. Leadership.
4. Commercial Awareness.

ACHIEVEMENT DRIVE

What it is:
'...is the inner drive to do things better, to meet and exceed targets, to strive for excellence and continuous improvement'

Why it matters:
Profitable growth is the primary purpose for Air UK. Being committed to consistent long-term growth in earnings and superior returns for our shareholders. We must grow our business whilst having a consistent focus on costs and productivity.

It is vital to focus on the achievement of our Strategic Targets and not get sidetracked. We must be proactive in making things happen and championing changes within our organisation.

This competency is demonstrated through the ability and willingness to work hard and to take responsibility for achievement and exceeding personal targets. There must be a commitment to excellence in everything we do. A company-wide ethos of excellence is necessary. The aim of everybody should be to simply be the best - to aspire always to give excellent performance. It is crucial that personal targets are aligned to Strategic Targets and are freely communicated to colleagues.

What it isn't:

- Being easily sidetracked from important targets.
- Consistently under achieving in personal targets.
- Starting projects enthusiastically but quickly losing interest without seeing things through.
- Taking failure personally, being slow to recover from disappointments.

ACHIEVEMENT DRIVE – BEHAVIOURAL INDICATORS

1. **Meets Targets:**
   - acknowledges the importance of targets and seeks to achieve them
   - works to meet targets set by others - delivers what is required
   - expresses dissatisfaction or frustration at inefficiencies without doing, or being able to do, much about it

2. **Wants to do well:**
   - sets own targets and works to meet them
   - expresses satisfaction at being asked to do a difficult task - rises to a challenge
   - seeks feedback on and works to improve own capability

3. **Improves performance:**
   - pushes to do things better
   - takes pride in what has been achieved, but always seeks to improve things even further
   - sees obstacles as challenges and enjoys overcoming them
   - sets standards/targets beyond those required and continually strives to achieve them

4. **Strives to be the best:**
   - sets out to be the best - has own measures of excellence and seeks feedback
   - takes calculated risks, after weighing up all the options, in order to improve performance
   - sets challenging business targets which reflect key strategic priorities
   - agrees and sets stretching targets for staff which may involve an element of risk taking.

Figure 3.6 An example of an Air UK competency

How competencies are used in development and succession planning

Very recently, all senior posts in the company have been job evaluated using the Hay system. Part of this system requires the post to be evaluated for competency levels required. Once this has been done (not yet) managers and supervisors will be able to see the level of competency required in the job, compare that with the competency level achieved by the staff member and then use the gap – if there is one – as the development opportunity. The Personnel Department has an HR database (PWA) that is capable of matching competencies of the job with those owned by staff.

The 'dictionary of competencies' is a document open to all staff through the IT network. In it the full description of all competencies is outlined. This means that staff are able to see what is entailed in moving from one competency level to the next. Those staff wishing to move jobs in the company can then direct their energies into developing their competencies to assist their career plans. Once the 'Business excellence system' is introduced, the intention is to make available all job profiles to all staff through the IT network.

Job family progression through different competency levels

'Job family' in this context means a logical series of jobs that staff might progress through in their overall career with the company. For example the customer services department has the following jobs with the competency levels required for each level clearly stated:

- Customer service agent
- Senior customer service agent
- Customer service supervisor
- Duty manager
- Airport manager.

By defining the career path and by clearly establishing the required competency levels for each stage of the development process, staff are in a good position to see what levels they have to achieve to progress in the organization. The appraisal exercise is then the opportunity to discuss and agree how higher competency levels can be achieved. This could be through job rotation, mentoring, training, etc.

Competencies as part of performance management

Air UK's approach is to consider competencies as just one element of the performance management process in the airline. To gain an impression of how competencies fit into the overall picture within Air UK, please refer to Figure 3.5.

The 'Business excellence system' is designed to ensure that all the elements of the European model of total quality management are a normal part of the management process in Air UK:

- leadership
- policy and strategy
- people management
- resources
- processes
- customer satisfaction
- people satisfaction
- impact on society
- business results.

From Figure 3.5 it can be seen that critical points for competencies are:

- appraisal carried out with competency levels noted
- personal development plan set (based on competency requirements)
- management development carried out
- competency matching of candidates
- succession plan drawn up.

Technology

One of the main objectives of the 'Business excellence' approach is to create the paperless office. Not only is this important in environmental terms, but by using IT effectively, people become much more involved in the whole process.

Air UK is undergoing a major investment programme by re-equipping with personal computers. Within a relatively short time, they will have some 350 PCs connected through the Air UK network. Following this investment programme, these 350 PCs will be located in each one of the company's bases and staff will have access into the 'Encyclopaedia of work'. For senior staff it is intended that not only will their job profiles be stored in the system but also their appraisals, using the job profile as the source document.

For all staff the 'Encyclopaedia of work' will be made available. This will mean that they will be able to access all competency definitions, all company sponsored training courses and all work processes for the company. In this way, they can have much greater control of the direction of their own careers. By seeing what is entailed in a job (job profile and work processes), by studying the competency levels required and by looking at the dictionary of competencies, they can work out what needs to be achieved. Finally, by going through the various company sponsored training courses, they can get an idea of how to achieve the next competency level.

Summary

Using a competency-based approach to developing staff will make an impression in a company. However, competencies on their own are but a small part of an integrated human resource programme. With today's technology, companies must integrate a competency approach with the other elements of good people management.

The 'Business excellence system' such as is used in Air UK provides progressive companies with an ideal opportunity to develop people policies that will add value to the organization as well as making a difference to how staff and managers interrelate.

Air UK's 'dictionary of competencies' is a similar concept to that used by other large organizations. Other case studies in this and my previous books outline examples of the development of a 'competence bank' which was then used to profile roles across the organization. London Fire and Civil Defence Authority (page 58) and MCL Group (page 78) also adopt methods which allow change to be led by a competence-based structure in this way.

A further example, but with some different components, can be found in the BUPA case study (see page 72).

3.2 BUSINESS-LED COMPETENCE FRAMEWORKS

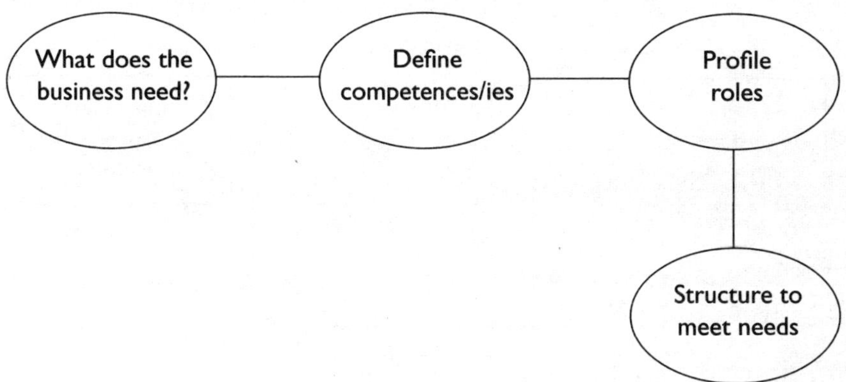

Figure 3.7 Business-led competence

Perhaps one of the most important aspects to keep in mind when developing a competence framework is that it must be *business-led*.

If a framework is developed by looking solely at individuals or their roles, the competences/ies defined will reflect the individual/role perspective. However, if development is approached first and foremost from the aspect of business needs, then what the business needs *leads* the development of that framework (see Figure 3.7). This also suggests that required competences/ies lead flexibility in organization structure, which in turn leads change.

The 'who' component of human resource functions must be secondary if an effective framework is to be developed and implemented (see Chapter 4). This is not to suggest that people are not important! On the contrary it suggests that people are a major resource and how this resource is developed and applied is critical to success.

As David McCammon, HR Director at Air UK, has outlined in the previous case study, competencies are just one component of the performance management process. Nevertheless, they are a key starting point. It is difficult to establish systems, procedures, processes and operations without clear expectations of performance at all levels.

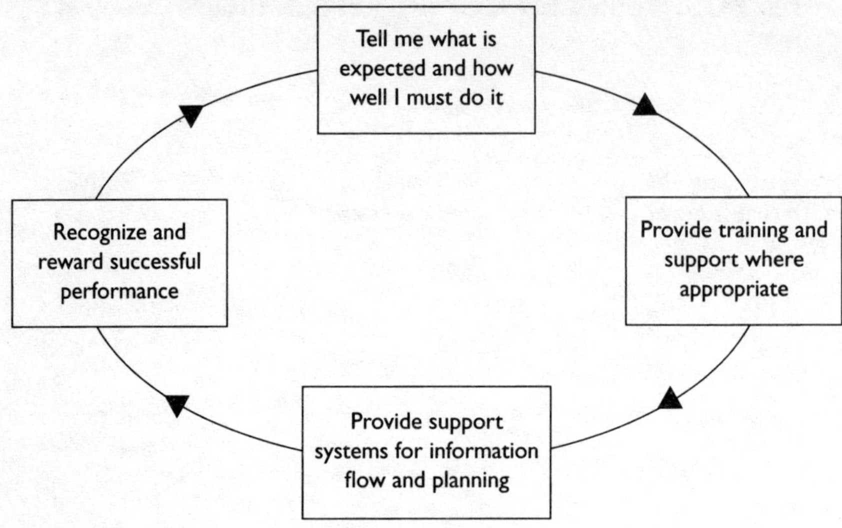

Figure 3.8 Setting and agreeing clear expectations of performance

As Figure 3.8 illustrates, for the individual within any organization clear expectations of performance are a critical starting point for performance management. Without these, other aspects have no foundation or reference point. The same model applies to department, division and strategic levels of a business organization. This is confirmed yet again in the ICL case study (page 101), the BUPA case study (page 72) and that from the MCL Group (page 78).

A move away from financial indicators

Traditional measures of business performance have been financial – profitability, earnings per share, and return on capital employed (ROCE). It is now becoming clear to many organizations that short-term financial measures alone are not good indicators of the health of the organization. 'New' measures include:

- quality
- customer satisfaction
- employee satisfaction.

A recent enquiry by the Royal Society of Arts, *Tomorrow's Company: The role of business in a changing world* (1995), called for companies to adopt measurement frameworks which incorporated 'financial components, but also feedback on the values, the health of key relationships and the performance of key processes within the business'.

The balanced score card – integrated performance measurement

As outlined in an earlier chapter (page 35) and in the BUPA case study (page 72), the 'balanced score card' is becoming increasingly popular among businesses as a means of using both financial and non-financial measures of performance, and providing a tool for integrated performance measurement.

The balanced score card (Kaplan and Norton, 1996) is a tool for assessment of organizational performance from four different perspectives, as Figure 3.9 indicates. The balanced score card approach

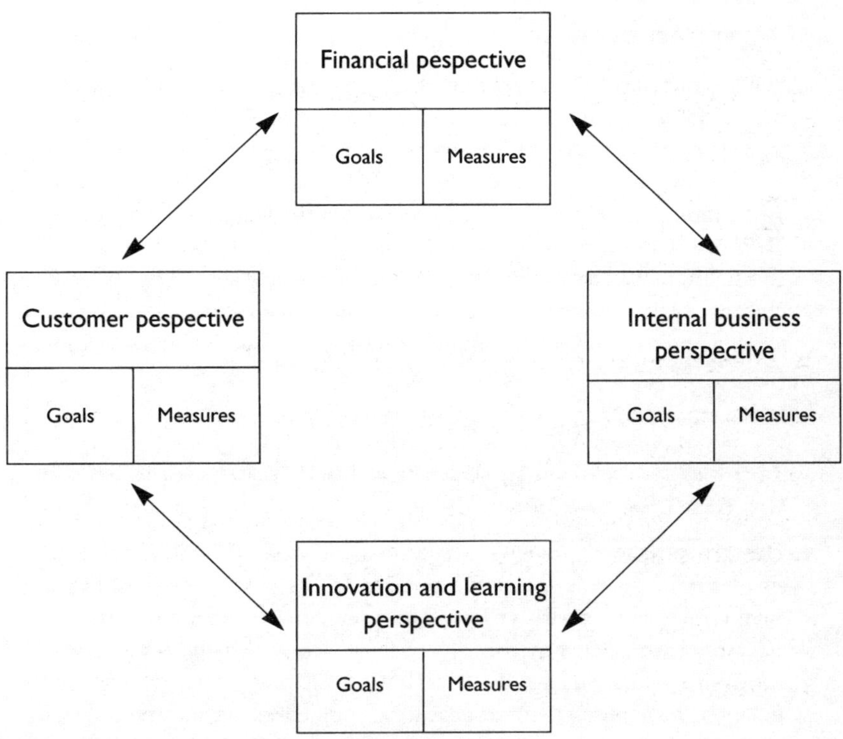

Figure 3.9 Balanced score card (Kaplan and Norton, 1996) adapted from the BUPA Project

focuses on long-term performance. In using the model, organizations must define a small number of key indicators for each perspective. These indicators must reflect the goals contained in the corporate vision. For each perspective, targets must be set with a specified period for achievement.

The use of measures in this way allows organizations to assess whether improvement in one area has been at the expense of another. By linking the Balanced Score Card with a competence framework, individual and group performance can be linked directly to business measures of success. This is illustrated in the following case study from BUPA.

■ CASE STUDY ■

BUPA

Organization details

BUPA is not only the leading private health company in the UK, it is also the world's only truly 'global' player, offering services in over 170 countries. It employs over 12,000 people and has a turnover well in excess of 1 billion, yet since its creation in 1947 it has remained a provident association – using its surpluses to reinvest in the health of its members. BUPA UK and International are the two main operating divisions, and in Great Britain people working in both divisions are served by one HR function. BUPA operates diverse businesses from insurance to hospitals, nursing homes to health screening, occupational health services to franchising health clubs, and many more.

The key issues facing the organization for the future – the need for change

Our group vision – BUPA's pre-eminent knowledge and experience enables it to provide the best solutions for its customers' healthcare needs – like many, clearly relies on our people to make it a reality. The main issue we faced was concern over our collective ability to deliver our strategy. Did we have the knowledge, skills and attitudes necessary and were we applying them to deliver our objectives? At the end of 1995 we had no idea, nor did we have a way of finding out or keeping track of our ability to deliver. Were we becoming more or less able, and why? A secondary issue was the proliferation of approaches to measuring ability and performance – the inheritance of multiple HR departments within organization structures which were united within the UK in 1995.

The organization change needed – what had to change

Primarily we had to find a way to systematically assess ability, and do so on a consistent basis over time. More specifically, we needed to agree standard definitions and methodologies, undertake an organization-wide review of the ability/competence requirements, and find a way to capture data about competency levels and track it over time. A big change for BUPA, and the greatest challenge, would be to find an approach that everyone would adopt. (BUPA's diversity is renowned internally for abandoning such efforts on the drawing board.)

Plans for change – how would change happen?

The critical success factors would be:

- an absolutely solid approach to competencies, their definition, assessment, validation and development
- full involvement and participation across the organization, particularly from people involved in the 30 or more competency projects/processes already underway
- an IT solution to the data capture and reporting requirement, linked to the performance management process for ongoing assessment
- cast iron project management and focus from the project team and steering group.

An aggressive timescale was set – one year to get the first cut of baseline competency level data across BUPA, representing our 'balance sheet of competency', against which we would measure profit and loss over time.

Process of change – what we did

We assigned a core team of two full-time employees, and contracted with an experienced consultant to provide guidance and resource where necessary. We started three months late due to other demands on time, but focused on the involvement/buy-in steps in the plan, keeping the senior management informed and getting a handle on the current situation in the organization. Competency definition workshops then began, along with system development and training planning, and then delivery. We reviewed off-the-shelf systems, but because of the importance of meeting the needs expressed within the consultation process we had little choice but to develop a bespoke solution.

The programme was driven by the need to understand, measure and develop competence, so it really was the central focus of the whole project.

Managing the change

Finding a way to make it happen was the task of the head of organization development, within the HR function. An OD officer project managed full-time and a steering group representing key parts of the organization met monthly to agree the plan and major decisions. There was a 'strategic' management drive in the form of BUPA's HR strategy which incorporated the programme, and our balanced score card which, among other things, tries to measure the development of our abilities within the company. Each line manager and other employee has a role to understand and manage the use of competencies – this was agreed by the steering group as one of the key sub-objectives of the project.

Bridges and barriers to change – problems/solutions

Bridges

- The fact it was a strategic objective, not just an HR thing
- high levels of understanding and predisposition in a number of key areas
- a credible steering group
- strong IT project management and excellent programming outsourcing
- commitment from the HR director.

Barriers

- An organization already trying to achieve many other very challenging objectives
- other agenda – differing systems/methods being developed elsewhere
- the ability of the IT infrastructure to handle an advanced Lotus Notes application, eg, PCs without pentium processors were slow
- lack of predisposition to performance manage in some areas.

Achievements of change – were objectives met?

By June 1997 we had standard methodologies, a great computerized performance management system, a 50 per cent complete competency framework, trained but not experienced people, and a balance sheet for our top three levels of management. We had linked competencies into our succession planning, recruitment, training and some change management initiatives (eg, to define changed behavioural characteristics). We were able to assess our strong and weak competencies at senior management level and plan development. But we have not yet validated the competency framework on the judgements people are making, and we have not yet driven recruitment/development activity to address competency deficits. All this and much more is to follow. By the end of 1997 we will have online data about competency levels of thousands of BUPA employees and the processes in place to measure gains or losses in competence, and overall validate against our ability to deliver our strategy.

With the benefits of hindsight – what would we have done differently?

Started sooner. Not tried to do so much so fast. Piloted completely in several different areas, over several years!

Though not conscious of it at the time, we adopted a fairly comprehensive approach to change, incorporating aspects of rational/empirical, normative/re-educative, and contextual perspectives. We majored on rationality, reverted to 'hearts and minds' when confronted with apathy or lack of commitment, and always mentioned the inescapability of the whole thing because it was a requirement of our ISO 9002 quality system and needed for the balanced score card!

Competence model adopted

We defined competency as, 'Ability applied to achieve specific outcomes', and elaborated with, 'A competent person applies knowledge, skill and attitude, and associated behaviours, at work, to meet specified standards'. Our competencies have positive and negative behavioural indicators, and the frequency of effective positive behaviour whenever it is needed is the basis of the rating scale. We also provide guidance on the outcomes/hard evidence likely to result from frequent effective positive behaviours as an aid in assessment, and lists of the knowledge, skills and attitudes needed to enable positive behaviour. The competencies are developed using versions of functional or process analysis, repertory grid technique and critical incident analysis, and will be validated by correlations with performance against business objectives. A framework including personal (for all), management, functional/job, and strategic (collective) competencies has been developed.

Other tools for measurement

The implementation of BUPA's competence framework continues with further role profiling to be undertaken.

The use of the mixed financial/non-financial measures used in the balanced score card and the flexibility of a business-led competence framework provide a valuable business tool. Other, similar models have been adopted, for example, the 'Performance pyramid' (Lynch and Cross, 1995). This approach has four integrated levels that concentrate on external effectiveness and internal efficiency, again flowing from the corporate vision.

The internal focus includes the traditional financially-based measures and the external focus involves a customer satisfaction quality. The apex of the pyramid is the organization's goals and corporate strategy; at its base are performance measures.

Further information on this approach and on the use of integrated performance management systems by organizations such as London Underground, Forte Hotels, Skandia Life and Bass Taverns can be found in the *IRS Management Review*, Issue 5, April 1997. As the conclusion of this publication states, 'Performance measurement is undergoing something of a transformation'.

Summary

With a greater focus on the non-financial and less traditional aspects of performance at business level, a competence framework can be used to its full potential.

This potential includes facilitating culture change, business growth and continuous improvement processes as illustrated by the case studies in the following sections.

3.3 COMPETENCE AND BUSINESS GROWTH

Introduction

Changes in the business environment and external influences on operations require changes in expectations of people performance and in role structure. When market changes create new business opportunities, this restructuring or expansion of competences must take place in a short-time scale – before the opportunity disappears.

In the following case study, Mazda Cars, part of the MCL Group, had to respond quickly to new opportunities. A great and different focus on customers was needed across the company; the sales function needed to be able to respond to a large increase in potential market. The 'people component' of the business was given strategic importance with the recognition that it would be people who make the change. Changes at senior management level also meant a change in style – all adding up to a requirement for 'culture change'.

This type of 'discontinuous' change (Drucker, 1969) is common in today's business environment, as evidenced by publications such as *Thriving on Chaos* (Peters, 1988) and *The Age of Unreason* (Handy, 1990). Key aspects of this type of change are business tools such as team-building, adhocracy, project management, cross-functional working and mentoring.

Communication at all levels becomes an essential aspect of performance management and this communication depends on a 'common language' of expectations.

Mazda decided to use nationally devised UK standards of performance as a starting point but needed to ensure flexibility of use and direct integration with corporate objectives. Competence profiling was therefore an essential component of success for the future with the resulting structure providing a basis for grading, reward, mobility and flexibility of operations at all levels.

Company-specific competencies are also a component of the new, integrated performance management system. A further interesting aspect of this case study is outlined in Sally Vanson's comments on 'bridges and barriers' to change, where she refers to the 'comfort zone' experienced by some employees and the influence of this experience on initial stages of introduction.

■ CASE STUDY ■

MAZDA CARS (UK) LTD

Organizational Details

Mazda Cars UK Ltd imports from Japan and distributes Mazda cars throughout the UK via a network of 150 franchised dealerships. The company is situated In Tunbridge Wells, Kent, and currently employees in the region of 110 employees, outsourcing support functions such as human resources financial accounting, etc to the parent company, MCL Group.

Key issues

In the past two years, the company has gone through a period of change, mainly brought about by increased market share. There has also been a change of MD at group level, and the recruitment of new sales and marketing directors into Mazda in 1996 injected an increase in pace. Ford took management control of Mazda Motor Corporation in Japan in 1996 and have an expectation of increased sales in Europe over the next three years.

Organizational change

In order to cope with the opportunities and push for business growth through increased volume, a far greater focus on customer orientation and personal accountability was required. There was a need to focus on the skills of employees in a greater way than ever before, and to ensure they were given the development needed to take the business forward. There had to be an understanding of the part that each and every one would play in this, allowing a shift in the critical behaviours displayed to customers both internal and external.

Plans for change

The main board in conjunction with MMC (Mazda Motor Corporation, in Japan) decided to plan for incremental growth over a period of three years. They also agreed that for the first time human resource development would feature at strategic level in the business planning activities and this would require the recruitment of a group HRD manager and a framework for the development of people, with an initial focus on performance management and customer orientation.

Sally Vanson was recruited as group HR development manager in April 1996. Investors In People was agreed as the framework for the change management process and commitment to the standard was made in September 1996.

As part of this commitment, initial investigations were made into the performance management system, as a measure of individual contribution to the key performance indicators of Mazda. Although work objectives were reasonably well set in SMART terms, the focus was on output and not the process of achievement. The downside of this was that it had emanated from the days when business planning had a one-year horizon, and was not geared to sustainable growth. Changes were made to the system to incorporate personal behavioural objectives and continuous improvement objectives which were either individual or team based, but this led to a further concern regarding individual measurement and development.

Research was done internally, among the franchise dealer staff and the end users of Mazda cars, to identify what critical behaviours employees should exhibit in order to enhance the customer relationship. Employees then completed questionnaires and attended workshops to identify their personal gaps against seven critical areas. The next step was about development to fill the gaps, measurement of progress and the ability of the line manager to know when the gap was filled.

The role of competence in the change programme

It gradually became apparent that a system of personal development and assessment was required that started by looking at job roles and task analysis in line with business objectives and followed through a recruitment, selection and development route that would support rather than interrupt business progress, and that would allow for objective assessment of individuals' skills and knowledge as well as personal behaviours. This programme would need to be flexible, to change and grow with the demands of the business and the employees and allow for internal and external benchmarking in an oversupplied and increasingly competitive market.

The corporate objectives of customer orientation and management accountability were revisited, and after investigation it was decided that occupational standards were the way forward. The pilot project was set up using the Customer Service Level 2 and 3 units and the Assessor Verifier Awards. The project was outsourced to Fletcher Consultancy on the strict understanding that it should not involve any bureaucratic paper chase and that achievement of relevant units of competence was to be the focus rather than full NVQs.

This move to competence-based development and assessment, and a link to the performance review system, allowed managers to see the relationship between the Assessor Verifier units and the appraisee and appraiser, confirming appraiser relationship. The performance criteria in the units enabled employees to be objectively assessed against the process of their achievements, rather than the end result which in the past could have been by luck rather than focused effort.

The use of the Customer Service units led to peer, subordinate and customer feedback, as well as that of the line manager, thus paving the way to a more open culture involving 360 degree feedback. The need to evaluate improvements to service allowed employees to put ISO 9000 into the business context rather than leave the formal file on the shelf, and the acknowledgement of internal customers assisted with the internal team-building needed to take major growth forward.

The whole system provided managers with an opportunity to start coaching their people in an informal, naturally occurring way, and employees started to reflect on their performance on a continuous basis rather than waiting for a formal review.

Who manages the change?

The change was initially driven by the directors, went through a period of being abdicated to the HRD manager, but was then taken back by the line managers and the employees themselves as the realization dawned that helping customers was easy and they felt good about themselves when they achieved success.

Bridges and barriers to change

The initial move to competence was regarded with suspicion, especially by those long-serving employees who were enmeshed in a comfort zone. There were also negative vibes from graduates who felt they had achieved all that was necessary and did not need continuous assessment in their roles. The bad press regarding NVQs worked against the project, especially when well intentioned people tried to match the levels against academic qualifications.

The pace at which the business was moving and the extra strain this put on staff did not help, and a lot of time was expended helping individuals to understand the need to maintain quality even when under pressure, and that this was the best opportunity to demonstrate competence and exhibit positive behaviours.

The language/jargon of the units was not generally user-friendly and as employees wrestled with it, the cultural change moved back a step before it went forward. The internal assessors tended to opt out and the HR development manager had to spend a lot of time on one-to-one coaching and feedback.

The bridges to success were via those candidates who achieved quickly being able to share their success and through the use of external assessors to kick-start and support the system. Very slowly, candidates started to take responsibility for their own assessment and this set them on the road to accountability.

Achievements of change

Rome was not built in a day! The change is happening slowly. Employees are gaining confidence, learning to trust and communicate more. The 'box mentality' is slowly being broken down and staff are starting to work in a more integrated fashion.

This small introduction of competence-based development and assessment is leading to the profiling and introduction of management and technical competences and a 360 degree feedback system. Directors have been trained as assessors; the performance review system is better managed; and in 1998 competences will flow from personal objectives.

Culturally employees are moving forward in a united fashion; the business is still growing; and the franchise dealers are commenting on the motivation they get from seeing Mazda's own staff going through the initiatives that they are encouraging the dealer staff to take on board. The main achievement so far can be measured in terms of integration and unity.

With the benefit of hindsight

The introduction of customer service first was right, but the external assessment support should have been carried on throughout the first year. It slowed the process down, trying to introduce a fairly complex system into a rapidly expanding business, and a more directive external approach, would have reaped faster results.

Model of change

A traditional model:

Commit → Communicate → Gain support → Communicate → Plan
Communicate → Implement → Communicate → Review and refine
Communicate → Evaluate → Communicate → Broaden

Competence model adopted

The next steps are to complete profiles for a further 400 employees across the group, providing a profiling report linking competences to roles/levels as a tool for future career/succession planning, evaluation and review (see Figure 3.10).

Critical Behaviours	**Management Behaviours**	**Core Management Competences**	**Core Customer Related Competences**
	Planning and organising	Plan and prepare projects	Plan and organise personal working schedule
Following through	Leadership	Control of running projects	Contribute to effective working
	Resilience	Close out projects	Contribute to the collection and use of marketing information in order to meet sales
Tactical	Problem solving and analysis and specialist knowledge	Meet customer requirements	Solve problems on behalf of customers
Technical	Creating and innovation	Implement change and improvement in organisational activities	Initiate and evaluate change to improve service to customers
Structuring	Strategic and commercial awareness	Determine effective use of resources	Maintain reliable customer service
Quality Focus	Quality orientation and personal motivation	Enhance own performance	Communicate with customers
Customer Focus	Persuasiveness	Enhance productive working relationships	Develop positive working relationships with customers
	Oral and written communication	Chair and participate in meetings	Contribute to effective working
	Interpersonal sensitivity	Assess competent performance	Assess competent performance
	Flexibility	Assess competent performance using diverse evidence	
Sales Focus	Action orientation	Identify and generate selling opportunities	Identify and generate selling opportunities

Figure 3.10 (reproduced with permission of MCL Group)

Summary

Organization values and the drive for success must be reflected in culture, and culture can be developed by setting and communicating clear objectives, measures and expectations.

In a review of 17 organizations covering different sectors, all of which were experiencing and/or aiming for culture change, it was found that there are three broad reasons why an organization might want to mount a culture change (*IRS Management Review*, January 1997, Volume 1, Number 4, Page 3):

- the existing culture may no longer be appropriate to changing business circumstances
- the existing culture's strength may inhibit the capacity to respond to change
- even where culture change is not the primary aim of a change programme it may nonetheless inhibit progress.

The same study identified key influences on decisions to start culture change; these included 'competitive pressures', government policies, customer focus and quality initiatives.

3.4 COMPETENCE AND INNOVATION

TGI Friday's is a fast-growing enterprise and has considerable experience in the use of its own competence frameworks. It has a major focus on customer excellence, taking a broad view of customer satisfaction, which incorporates not only customer contact, but the environment, quality service and quality products.

■ CASE STUDY ■

TGI FRIDAY'S

TGI Friday's is operated in Britain by Whitbread Restaurants & Leisure, a division of Whitbread plc. Whitbread is licensed to operate the franchise in the UK on behalf of TGI Friday's Inc. The first TGI Friday's opened in New York in 1965. Sales in the first year exceeded $1 million and the concept has become one of America's most famous eating places. Whitbread brought it, unaltered, to Britain in 1986.

There are currently 23 restaurants in Britain. TGI Friday's employs approximately 148 managers and 2200 staff. Plans include doubling its size by 2001.

History

The original restaurant boasted the same red and white striped awnings, wooden flooring, Tiffany lampshades, bent-wood chairs and striped table cloths retained in today's restaurants. An immediate success, TGI Friday's became hugely popular with young New Yorkers, quickly becoming *the* place to meet.

In 1971 a group of Dallas businesses franchised a TGI Friday's (Friday's) in Dallas. Before opening the restaurant they spent six months looking for antiques with which to decorate it. Stained glass windows, rocking horses, wooden aeroplane propellers, racing sculls and metal advertising signs adorned the walls when the Dallas Friday's opened in 1972 – the 'elegant clutter' which remains one of Friday's famous features.

Again the restaurant was a huge success, netting record-setting sales of $2 million in its first year. The Dallas franchise joined with the New York Friday's to form TGI Friday's Inc. By 1975 there were ten restaurants in eight states, and the company was acquired by the Carlson Hospitality Group.

At this stage TGI Friday's conducted a comprehensive analysis of the reasons for its success. A number of functional theories and philosophies were crystallized and form the basic principles by which Friday's operates today.

Central to Friday's success was its ability to care for its guests. Anticipating and supplying their needs appeared to be the key to continuing that success.

Recognizing that a vital element of the restaurant's appeal is the atmosphere, Friday's created a comfortable, relaxing environment in which the customer could enjoy quality food and drink. Nothing was, or is, left to chance. Decor, music, lights, air-conditioning and housekeeping were all designed for the guests' comfort.

The company and its employees constantly examined and learned from customer feedback and experience. Employees learned to be more spontaneous and were encouraged to display their own personalities, treating customers as they would guests in their own homes. The menu and drinks list expanded to meet increasingly sophisticated customer requirements and Friday's innovative flair became apparent as it soared to become market leader.

Early innovations were appetizer potato skins and the popularization of nachos. It was the first restaurant chain to offer stone-ground wholewheat bread, avocados, bean sprouts and Mexican appetisers across the US.

It is considered by some that America owes the popularization of frozen and iced drinks to Friday's. It developed fruit-based, alcohol-free concoctions as well as its ever-growing portfolio of alcoholic drinks. So precise was the mixing of these drinks that the company commissioned the manufacture of tailor-made glasses which have since become industry standards.

TGI Friday's – the employer

One of the principal philosophies upon which Friday's bases its business is its triangle theory. A solid balance must be maintained between the guest, the employee and the company: upset the balance and the company fails to function efficiently.

Staff enjoy working at Friday's because they get job satisfaction, earn good money and have fun. As well as being well suited to their jobs, they are well trained, motivated and highly valued. Their enthusiasm rubs off on the guests, contributing to the restaurants' buzzing atmosphere where there is always something different going on.

Friday's record of staff retention illustrates the success of this theory. Members of the original team in the Birmingham restaurant still work there 11 years later, and other restaurants boast comparable success. The rapid expansion of the company offers ongoing opportunities to staff for promotion and progression on the management scale.

People are recruited for their attitude rather than traditional restaurant skills. These are people who take pride in their work and cheerfully give 110 per cent to make sure every guest enjoys their visit to Friday's, and will return.

Each restaurant employs approximately 90 staff, including waiters and waitresses, line cooks, bartenders, hosts and hostesses, office and maintenance staff, all supervised by a general manager and his or her team of managers.

TGI Friday's – the experience

Regular guests to Friday's talk about the Friday's experience – a mix of buzzing atmosphere, flamboyant decor and friendly staff with a real will to please.

Central to the Friday's concept is its emphasis on guest satisfaction. Staff treat guests as if they were valued visitors to their own homes. They are met at the door with a warm welcome and accompanied to their table in true Friday's style.

TGI Friday's UK competence framework for managers

Several years ago, TGI Friday's developed company-specific management competencies to be used as a tool for continuously improving management performance. The implementation process, which covered all management roles in the 23 UK sites, included production of the competencies in a ring-bound format which referenced these competences as 'Management keys'. Briefing on use of the competencies was provided for all managers, and included opportunities for role play where the competencies could be 'acted out' and assessment judgements explored.

The structure of the competence framework includes eight competencies at five levels, presented in a 'dimensions/clusters' format. Assessment of competence is undertaken through observation and review of actual performance and the outcomes recorded in the 'Management keys' booklet. Each manager must aim for an average score of 3.5 across the competencies. Formal reviews are undertaken twice a year on a fixed time basis. All assessment is undertaken by the relevant line manager.

A copy of the assessment record for each management key is retained by the manager. A further copy is sent to head office. The results of all assessments are reviewed and form the company training plan. In addition information is recorded on a personal game plan which the individual is responsible for achieving.

Achievement at levels and breadth of responsibility in management roles are also recognized by bronze, silver and gold pins. In addition, the 'Keys review' is linked to pay review, placing a focus on reward of demonstrated competence in a management role.

Competencies for other TGI Friday's employees

Current practice in assessment and review of hourly employee performance includes a six-monthly review which will ultimately be linked to career planning. Personal game plans are being introduced and training provided is recorded on store training records. Core training programmes are provided centrally with the use of cascade training for all employees.

Front-of-house employees are assessed against six generic competencies and one role-specific competence. These will be linked into the recruitment and review process over the next 12 months.

NVQs were tested for the hourly front- and back-of-house employees, but pilots were not successful. Difficulties with the structure and level of NVQs in this area were experienced and it was found that the content was too traditional for the upbeat and proactive market in which TGI Friday's operates. Similarly, the customer service NVQ was found to be at too basic a level and did not reflect the expectations of TGI Friday's in respect of contact with guests. TGI Friday's is, however, keeping an open mind on the NVQ front and will consider revisiting new standards and structures towards the end of 1997.

Current developments

TGI Friday's approach to manager and employee development focuses on motivation and reward. Anyone visiting a TGI Friday's store cannot fail to notice the pins and badges worn by all staff. Each of these has meaning in terms of recognition of performance – this recognition, and the support to continuously achieve and improve, will be an integral part of future plans.

A recent review and updating of TGI Friday's mission and values, in response to a changing market and new opportunities, mean a review of competencies. The 'Management keys' will be updated and the new mission and values incorporated. These have already been included in the new employee competencies.

3.5 COMPETENCE AND EMPLOYEE DEVELOPMENT

Organizations planning competence-based performance management systems need to consider carefully what type of competence framework to use.

Sheffield City Council decided to make use of the UK national standards with the system of NVQs to assist with their change programme. The following case study emphasizes the need *actively* to recognize the importance of people and of linking people performance to business performance.

■ CASE STUDY ■

SHEFFIELD CITY COUNCIL

Organizational details and background

Sheffield City Council is a large organization (approximately 21,000 employees) and one which is undergoing a considerable amount of change. It serves Sheffield's population of 528,000. The Council is made up of 87 elected members, each representing the people of Sheffield within various constituencies throughout the city.

The Authority is responsible for a full range of statutory and non-statutory services, for example, social services, housing, libraries, recreation, education, parks. The Council spends approximately £410 million (net) annually on services.

The Cleaning of Buildings DSO forms an integral part of Sheffield City Council's Cleansing Services Department. The DSO operates with an annual turnover of £4–5 million and employs 1200 cleaning operatives. Its service operations break down into a number of contracts:

1. The Sheffield non-schools cleaning premises contracts, eg town hall, libraries, housing offices, social centres.
2. The collective Sheffield comprehensive schools' cleaning contracts.
3. The primary and nursery school service level agreements.
4. A collection of individual short-term, non-contractual service level agreements, eg an agreement with the Housing Department to clean and clear vacant housing properties.

Key Issues (the need for change)

The service has to submit competitive tenders for all its work and this process means that we need to have:

- skilled staff
- positive image
- a focus on quality.

Training methods need to be developed, not only in technical skills and knowledge, but also in terms of customer service. Linked to this, the service has recognized the need to improve its marketing and publicity techniques and ensure that its policies, procedures and documentation actually enable the delivery of a quality service.

There are also greater demands being placed on us by our customers who, in their attempt to achieve value for money, are asking more questions and commanding more precise and detailed information about our service.

Plans for change/process of change and the role of competence

In a climate of constant change, the service found itself in the middle of a major review of Council services, with the reduction in directorates from 15 to five. Given this, and the key issues facing the Department, Cleaning of Buildings recognized the need to take some action to move the service forward.

A focus on more specific customer requirements was also required; for example, the special needs schools in Sheffield asked for the development of a specific training programme for cleaning operatives allocated to their schools.

We knew that the key to success was to focus on the front-line staff who actually provide the service. Careful thought was given as to how we might go about identifying the development needs of the workforce, while at the same time recognizing their existing skills and experience. The options were discussed with the City Council's training section and it was agreed that the best way forward was to use the National Standards and vocational qualifications for the cleaning industry. This approach would not only provide staff with a national qualification but would benefit both the Department and its customers in terms of image and quality of service.

The NVQ programme was introduced to provide an overall improvement in the competence of the workforce. The process was implemented particularly to create a greater understanding of the roles of the cleaning operatives and to focus more clearly on areas of customer service and satisfaction.

At the same time we planned to use the Standards to help develop the effectiveness of both the induction training package and staff training generally. They would also assist in the development and writing of the service's quality document and in improving communication links with both staff and clients.

Specifics

It was decided to choose an area of service where there would be clear potential benefits. The cleaning contract for comprehensive schools was due for renewal so it was felt that this was an appropriate area to pilot the project.

To make it manageable, ten schools were selected, involving approximately 120 cleaners and ten on-site supervisors who would both support and assess them. This would also enable us to reflect on and learn from the experience before looking at a wider implementation. Given our relative inexperience in this area, it was agreed to work in partnership with Sheffield College, using their resources and expertise.

A timescale of 12 months was agreed to review and evaluate the project.

Managing the change

Initially the change was driven by the enthusiasm of an Assistant Director of the service. There was also a political influence, with support from a number of Sheffield councillors who encouraged and supported the idea of time and effort being invested in the workforce at ground level.

The project itself was administered by an activity manager working in this area and the secondment of a supervisor/trainer who took on the roles of NVQ Coordinator and Internal Verifier. Advice and support were obtained from the Council's in-house training division which has proved to be an important factor in keeping the project on course.

Good communication became essential for the success of the pilot project, and all the customers, cleaning supervisors and cleaning operatives involved were spoken to and kept informed of progress on a regular basis.

Bridges/barriers – problems and solutions

There were a number of problems to overcome both prior to the commencement of the project and throughout the NVQ programme:

1. There was difficulty in informing and changing the 'thinking' of both the customers and the cleaning operatives so that everyone was aware of what the NVQ programme was attempting to achieve.
2. Producing and writing the appropriate working documentation

became a lengthy task, particularly as the NVQ requirements did not fit comfortably with our existing culture.

3. Communicating across a wide range of sites and personnel proved to be a challenge. Informing politicians, senior management officers and school headteachers of a 'new' concept took a considerable amount of time. Underpinning this challenge were the geographical splits of the premises where these personnel were based.
4. A separate challenge was the development of a new and quite different working relationship with the Sheffield College. Cleaning of Buildings' employees had little knowledge of NVQ programmes prior to commencement of the scheme. Similarly, the project proved to be a quite a different development approach for members of the Sheffield College. Consequently, some initial problems occurred while the relationship between the two separate organizations was being developed.
5. Another difficulty was seeking the additional funding required to initiate the programme. As a large DSO, Cleaning of Buildings operates within the constraints of compulsory competitive tendering and so any attempts to obtain extra funds became very difficult.
6. Finally, it was decided that the on-site cleaning supervisors, based at comprehensive schools, would become NVQ Assessors. These supervisors had the task of assessing and supervising staff as well as helping to clean large areas. Therefore, they required a substantial amount of support, especially in the early stages of the project.

Despite these barriers, most of the problems were overcome and the solutions developed as follows:

1. To commence the project it was necessary to put aside plenty of time for planning and discussion. In particular, informing all the customers in detail about the likely long-term benefits of the training programme was vital. Also, enthusiasm among the cleaning operatives and gaining their respect and trust were very important. Time spent on choosing the first ten schools for introduction into the scheme was time well spent. Schools with experienced staff and stable working environments were highlighted for the pilot phase. Essentially, this pre-planning stage was the catalyst for the future success of the programme.
2. Allocating responsibilities and specific time to members of the administration team working on the programme was also successful. Ensuring good communication throughout the department and the college was important. Weekly communication with customers, supervisors and senior management helped to ensure the effective running of the programme.
3. The problems relating to the additional funding requirements were

solved by 'selling' the principles underpinning the project to the Sheffield councillors and senior management. In particular, it was emphasized that the Council would be seen to be investing in manual staff working on front-line services. This became the key issue for eventually attracting the funding.

4. The cleaning supervisors based at the pilot schools became NVQ Assessors. A solution to relinquishing some of their duties was to remove the cleaning element from their daily schedules. In effect, this created ten non-cleaning supervisors/NVQ Assessors, which not only allocated them sufficient time to assess but also helped them to realize that there was genuine commitment to and belief in the programme from management.

Achievements of Change

The project is still in progress but a number of significant achievements have been made to date:

1. Relationships have developed and improved between supervisors (Assessors) and cleaners and between the mobile supervisor/trainer (Internal Verifier) and all staff.
2. There is a much better understanding of why and how tasks are done, eg the colour coding of cleaning materials is linked to health and safety and COSHH regulations; the wearing of overalls is as much to do with the image of the service and security as it is with protection.
3. It has helped to highlight the development needs of different supervisors, particularly in relation to their management role.
4. Improvements have been seen in the cleaners' knowledge and understanding as well as in their technical skills.

What would have been done differently?

A different mix of premises in the pilot project would have given a clearer indication of other issues and implementation problems in non-school sites, eg different usage, clients and cleaning specifications.

We would have looked carefully at the possibility of developing a team of peripatetic assessors with replacement mobile cleaners moving on to sites when NVQ assessment is taking place. This could make expansion of the project easier to manage.

Model of change/competence model adopted

The basic model adopted followed the NVQ assessment framework. The relevant National Occupational Standards and NVQs were selected, ie Cleaning of Building Interiors, Level 1.

Whenever possible, any training inputs required for cleaners are provided by the Cleaning Service's trainers on site, with college-based expertise being used when appropriate.

Sheffield College registered candidates through their Centre, giving the cleaners student status and therefore access to all the college facilities and resources.

3.6 COMPETENCE AND COMPETITION

The following case study from the Audit Commission illustrates the use of a competence framework to assist with response to a more competitive environment.

The expansion of compulsory competitive tendering (CCT) in the public sector, combined with agency restructuring in the last decade, has required a new focus in many organizations. As this case study states, organizations 'not only need to play the game better, they need to play a different game'.

■ CASE STUDY ■

AUDIT COMMISSION

Organizational details

The Audit Commission is a statutory body established in 1983. The Commission appoints external auditors to local authorities and NHS bodies in England and Wales. The auditors may be from its own arm's-length agency, District Audit (known as DA), or from private sector firms of accountants. The Commission determines fee scales payable by bodies and regulates the audits. It carries out studies of the economy, efficiency and effectiveness of services provided by audited bodies. It also specifies the indicators of performance which every local authority must collect and publish to facilitate the comparison of authorities' performance.

Most of the work of the auditors appointed by the Commission relates to two main areas:

- regularity and probity, which concerns the maintenance of proper books of account and the systems for ensuring honesty and integrity on the part of those responsible for public funds
- value for money in the provision of public services.

The Commission employs around 1300 staff of whom just over 1000 work within DA. In November 1994, DA became a free-standing agency, giving it new freedoms and responsibilities while remaining accountable to the Commission. This case study focuses on the changes in DA since November 1994 and the role of competence in that change.

Key issues/need for change

When DA was set up as an arm's-length agency in November 1994, there was a clear expectation from the Commission that DA needed to respond to the drive towards more competition across the public sector as a whole. Audited bodies were themselves faced with increased competition through, for example, CCT of some services. They were, in many cases, experiencing growing demand for services without a corresponding increase in income, so they were increasingly wanting more for less from their auditors. When those auditors were themselves preaching to the audited bodies about value for money and the three Es (economy, efficiency and effectiveness) this served only to increase the expectation that an authority's auditors would offer a high quality service at a competitive cost.

Audited bodies also had changed expectations of the nature of their relationship with their auditor. In delivering their own services, they were expected to become more responsive and 'citizen focused'. So, increasingly, they were demanding from their auditors a more proactive, two-way dialogue concerning the content, style and outcomes of the audit and were looking to be treated as clients or customers being provided with a service.

DA had to find a way of responding to this change while still fulfilling its traditional role as a watchdog, a role that required auditors to take issue with any authority they suspected of misspending the public purse.

Organizational change needed

DA needed to change in a fundamental way. To use a sporting analogy, it not only needed to play the game better, it also needed in some respects to play a different game. So, after around 150 years of successfully delivering public sector audit, it had to address some fundamental questions such as, 'what is an audit?'

To be able to answer these questions effectively, DA had to look both outwardly and inwardly. The outward look involved finding out the views of external stakeholders and identifying and learning from best practice in both the public and private sectors. The inward look involved taking stock of DA's long tradition and well established culture, deciding what was going to be of value for the future and planning to adapt or discard what was not. It also entailed an assessment of what was realistic, over what time-scale and at what cost.

Plans for change

The Audit Commission signalled the need for change in its five year strategy, 'Adding value', published in 1993. This defined in broad terms the new relationship with DA. It was followed by the development and publication of a framework document setting out how DA was to be managed at arm's length from the Commission in a structured purchaser/provider split. It established a panel of Commission members charged with the responsibility of ensuring that DA met its aims. The panel would be the link between a newly appointed chief executive of DA and the full Commission itself.

A more detailed picture of the way forward was presented in the first DA corporate plan in 1995. As well as setting out, as conventional wisdom demands, a mission and vision, the plan identified four key objectives, which were to:

- support the Audit Commission
- improve local audit
- develop market edge
- develop DA's people.

Against each of these objectives there were key change projects with milestones and targets for each. These change projects were later further refined into five critical success factors:

- *financial management* – ensuring that DA achieved its financial targets
- *reconciling expectations* – ensuring that the Commission and DA's clients had a common and accurate view of the quality of DA's work
- *market edge* – ensuring that DA established and maintained a lead over its competitors
- *key staff* – ensuring that high performance was rewarded and poor performance managed positively and effectively
- *aligning commitment and performance of all staff* – ensuring that staff were all working together towards the same objectives.

Process of change

In the three years since the plans were drawn up, there has been a process of continuing – some might say unremitting – change. It has largely followed the pattern set out above, although corporate plans and targets have been updated each year. In that time, DA has transformed not only what it does but also how it does it and how it manages itself.

There have been several key steps in the change process. First, there were significant changes at the top of DA. A new chief executive has been appointed. The District Audit Management Board has been enlarged and reorganized to include directors with responsibility for finance, business development and, perhaps most significantly, people development. The nature of the work and how it is now to be delivered have been defined formally in a quality manual. The new roles and ways of working were first piloted extensively and then adopted across the country. A performance management system has been introduced based on targets linked to the corporate plan. Changes to the line management structure, including some delayering, have been actioned. And in the last year, a new pay and grading system has been negotiated and implemented. Staff have had to acquire a whole range of new skills. Most have successfully made the transition from old to new ways of working. There have been no redundancies.

The role of competence in the change process

The concept of competence has been key to the whole change process. At an early stage, external consultants helped DA to look at the key competences that would be needed for the future. They interviewed not only key senior people but also a cross-section of staff at all levels. This produced a competence model with associated behaviours. Initially, many staff reacted adversely to the whole concept of a competence model, especially one which emphasized business and people skills as strongly as technical skills and knowledge. But the model, with some minor amendments, has proved remarkably resilient and relevant to the needs of DA over the last three years.

The competence model has been used primarily in the three key areas of selection, development and reward.

The **selection** of staff using a competence based approach has covered both recruitment and promotion and involved significant use of assessment centres. Over the three year period, this has resulted in a shift in emphasis in the key criteria for advancement away from just professional auditing skills to a matrix of auditing, business and people-related skills.

The **development** of new skills has been of paramount importance to DA in order for the change process to be successful. DA has introduced a personal development planning process based entirely on the competence model. Each year, every employee assesses his or her capabilities against the model and compares this with their boss's assessment. They then produce an action plan designed to address any mismatches between the desired and actual competence levels.

In order to achieve a clearer picture of development needs at both an individual and an organizational level, DA has run a series of development centres at the two key management grades of district auditor and audit manager. Despite many staff having initial fears and reservations, the centres have proved increasingly popular and successful. At the individual level, results have been fed into personal development plans. At the organizational level, results have influenced the nature and balance of DA's national training programme and have also highlighted areas where extra initiatives were needed to address significant organizational weaknesses.

In 1997, an extra element in the development process for managers is upward feedback, again based on the competence model.

DA's new **reward** system incorporates a process for progression through pay ranges which is competence based. The top part of each pay range is only available to those staff who are able to demonstrate excellence against a range of performance standards related to business outcomes. Rate of movement through the range is based on the speed with which an individual has added to their previous portfolio of these skills and has demonstrated them in work achievements.

The use of the competence model in these three key areas has resulted in a remarkable degree of acceptance that the skills and attributes in the model are, indeed, those necessary for individual and organizational success. Some staff may welcome this with open arms whereas others may lament (publicly or privately) the passing of an era when success was achieved by long service and technical competence alone. But all staff, virtually without exception, accept the model as representing a clear picture of what DA expects of its staff now and in the future.

Managing the change

It has been crucial to the success of the change process that it has been seen to be managed by the District Audit Management Board and, below them, by the Management Teams in the five DA regions. The key figures at the Board have been the chief executive and the director of people development. They have drawn on support from within the Audit Commission's own Human Resources function and from outside the organization where necessary. But all Board members have had a key role. 'Be the change you are trying to create' said Ghandhi; and all DA Board members have been expected to be role models for the new ways of working and managing.

Bridges and barriers to change

The biggest barrier to change has been the strength of the old culture, built up over many years in an organization where, typically, most staff joined at a young age and stayed until retirement. In that culture, many of the behaviours which had traditionally been rewarded were the opposite of those described in the new competence model. The old-style District Auditor, for example, was aloof from his clients (and, indeed, did not recognize them as being clients) and from his staff. If his clients and his staff held him in awe and feared his wrath, he would be highly regarded by his superiors.

Overcoming this barrier has not been easy, but the competence model has helped in setting out the behaviours desired for the future. The pressures for change both from the Commission and externally have also driven DA forward. Failure in an initial round of market testing of audits gave a very clear pointer to staff and management that reluctance to change was threatening the long-term viability of DA and the careers of its staff. Success in the next round of market testing after intensive training of the bid teams based on the core competence model demonstrated the way forward.

Achievements of change

Looking back at the objectives and critical success factors which DA set three years ago, there is no doubt that they have largely been met.

DA has succeeded in supporting the Commission, both by delivering its financial contribution and also by developing a mature relationship with the Commission as its owner. This relationship has recently been redefined in an updated framework document. DA has also delivered an improved local audit, as confirmed by client satisfaction reviews and by the internal quality review results. It can also claim to have developed its market edge, as measured by the results of market testing bids for new work. And it has certainly developed its people. This is demonstrated in particular by the results of development centres which show a closing of the gap between the desired and actual competence mixes.

It would be complacent to suggest that the change process is complete. The external world in which DA operates has not stood still over the last few years and clients are making new demands on DA. The change of government in May 1997 seems likely to produce further demands as the new regime adopts different policies for both local government and the health service. But the initial agenda has largely been delivered.

With the benefit of hindsight

There are many detailed parts of the change process which, with hindsight, would have been approached differently. But it is difficult to identify aspects of the overall plan that would have changed. Many of the time-scales set proved very demanding; but taking the change at a slower pace would only have increased the uncertainty for staff which has been one of the biggest downsides of the review. Along with other organizations, DA has not found the secret of how to take itself through a major change process without staff morale taking a severe dip along the way. If DA could have found the answer to that problem, it would certainly have been a formula worth applying.

Part of the morale problem has related to the difficulty of communicating effectively with staff who work in small teams on client premises.

When done well, face-to-face briefings from line managers have proved most effective. But this puts a great reliance on the commitment and communication skills of these managers. Communication was quite rightly identified as a key competence. But bringing all managers up to the required skills level has taken time; and in the interim, information has been in some instances less than effectively transmitted to staff, with a consequent effect on morale.

Model of change

The approach in DA owed something to the Kurt Lewin model of change as going from one steady state to another in a three-step process of unfreezing old attitudes, introducing change and then refreezing attitudes around the change. So there was a genuine attempt to create awareness of the need for change, to communicate honestly with people and to involve people in the change process. And now that the changes are in place, there is a focus on rewarding new behaviours that reinforce the new way of doing things. Lewin's model assumes that organizations return to a steady state after change. But in DA, as in most organizations, change seems to have become the norm.

Competence model adopted

It was an early decision that DA needed a bespoke competence suite rather than an 'off the peg' approach. So competences were developed based on an assessment of the future needs of DA combined with a process of structured interviews designed to explore perceptions of what differentiated high performers at each level from those who were perceived as being only satisfactory. The competences were identified and linked to their constituent behaviours. These were later developed into performance standards with business outcomes in such a way that the constituent parts linked together to form a whole picture of organizational competence.

Conclusion

Although the DA story is one of steady progress and ultimate success, it would only be honest to say that at many times over the period of change, it has been easier to see the problems rather than the progress.

A point has now been reached where some consolidation is ideally needed. But this may also be the time when DA will need to look at and refine its competence suite to gear itself up for the next three years in order to ensure its continuing success.

3.7 COMPETENCE AND PROACTIVE RESTRUCTURING

Changes in operations at ICL demanded a review of roles, competences and working interactions.

As the ICL case study states, changes in a competitive market mean that 'the product is not the computer, or the system, but the people who provide the computers and the services'.

■ CASE STUDY ■

ICL

With revenues of £2.4 billion in 1996 from continuing businesses, ICL is one of the top IT systems and services providers worldwide. Over the last five years, extensive restructuring has taken place. This included the merger of the Volume Products business with those of Fujitsu, creating one of the world's largest and most powerful PC suppliers. In addition, the sale of the contract manufacturing business, D2D, moved the core business into the IT systems and services market.

ICL employs 18,000 people internationally in several operating divisions, structured to respond to the needs of industry sectors. These divisions include the services operation which provides consultancy, outsourcing, training and networking; the maintenance operation; and main frame/server supply and distribution.

In 1996 ICL launched the precision retailing service. This gives retailers a greater understanding of their customers' purchasing habits and the facility to interpret and exploit this data through improved supply chain management, micro marketing and basket analysis. (Precision retailing is central to the WH Smith Club Card in the UK and has been taken up by Camelot Music and Stop & Shop in the US.)

ICL has provided integrated solutions for retail in-store applications and internet commerce, for financial services, for local and central government, for travel and media. This integrated approach is one which will become a key market for the future. In addition, ICL's outsourcing activities are in increasing demand, with 170 customers in the UK. Its global network spans 75 countries – a broad base which has enabled ICL's role in network management to expand with services including data, mail, voice, multimedia and call management.

ICL is a distributor, IT supply chain management company and reseller for over 400 manufacturers of PCDs, software, peripherals, printers and networks, including many of the leading brands. The company's ability to provide full and professional multi-vendor support and its reputation as the UK's top IT training company, by both market share and revenue, places it at the forefront of tailored, customer-driven business.

Key issues for the future

The nature of the business in which ICL operates is one of constant change. The restructuring of the business required a restructuring of roles and responsibilities. Employees needed new and broader skills, and roles which had to operate more flexibly across the organization. Integrated customer solutions require integrated human resource and operational strategies. People have to act differently if customers are to see ICL in its new role. There must, however, be commonality in the way people work, combined with specialization in sector. In a service business such as ICL now finds itself, the product is not the computer, or the system, but the people who provide the computers and the services. The wider range of competences and behaviours required by people mean that there are fewer types of people or roles, doing more things, and the business process must be led by customer need.

Plans for change

ICL recognized the importance of people competence and the impact that this will have on the business for the future. The need for people competence, and the requirement to restructure people roles have acted as catalysts for change. It is imperative to design a competence framework and to structure people roles around this. Motivation and reward need to be reviewed in different ways with a 'psychological contract' being developed as a working agreement. ICL decided that defining competences was a critical component for future success, and all human resource systems would be reviewed and updated based on this framework. The competence requirements of the organization would therefore lead the change required.

Planning and managing change

ICL found that the need for change had, in the past, been reactive. Attempts to tackle one aspect of change led to discussion on the impact of this on all other aspects of human resources and operations. The ultimate outcome of the discussions was that the required change project was 'too big'.

It was therefore decided to adopt a 'pilot' approach and start with divisions which had already recognized a need for change. As project work began, it was found that other work could be started as ideas and motivation developed alongside action for change. Work has been undertaken on defining competencies and new roles, establishing a psychological contract and management style.

ICL found that business changes are not possible without changes in human resource functions and systems.

Progress

ICL has completed about one-eighth of its original plan and has competencies in various drafts for some divisions. Further work is planned to address issues of how the competencies will be assessed and use of the framework within human resource functions such as reward, recruitment, training, appraisal, etc.

Bridges and barriers

With hindsight, ICL would adopt a top-down approach, gaining full senior management commitment for an organization-wide development. The use of champions is often a necessary step for many organizations but the need to start in one part of the organization can lead to the danger of repetition or reworking of a competence framework.

Many benefits are becoming apparent as the system develops. The use of a competence framework enables employees to see clearly what their role and expectations are and engenders a sense of worth. ICL has found that use of a competence framework also reduces attrition, by recreating an environment in which people can clearly establish their role as the 'right' person. In terms of business direction and success, ICL feels that use of a competence framework is enabling more control and proactivity, rather than being led by the past.

There is now a need to build on work undertaken and to establish a new culture by developing and modifying the framework to other divisions.

Approach to competencies

ICL has developed competencies for 'communities' (similar to job families). This approach avoids the hierarchical or vertical grading and succession planning pitfall by identifying competences across roles and the levels of complexity or responsibility that differentiate them. This facilitates a more flexible reward system – one of the initial driving forces for changing the human resource functions. An example of this 'community' is illustrated in Figure 3.11.

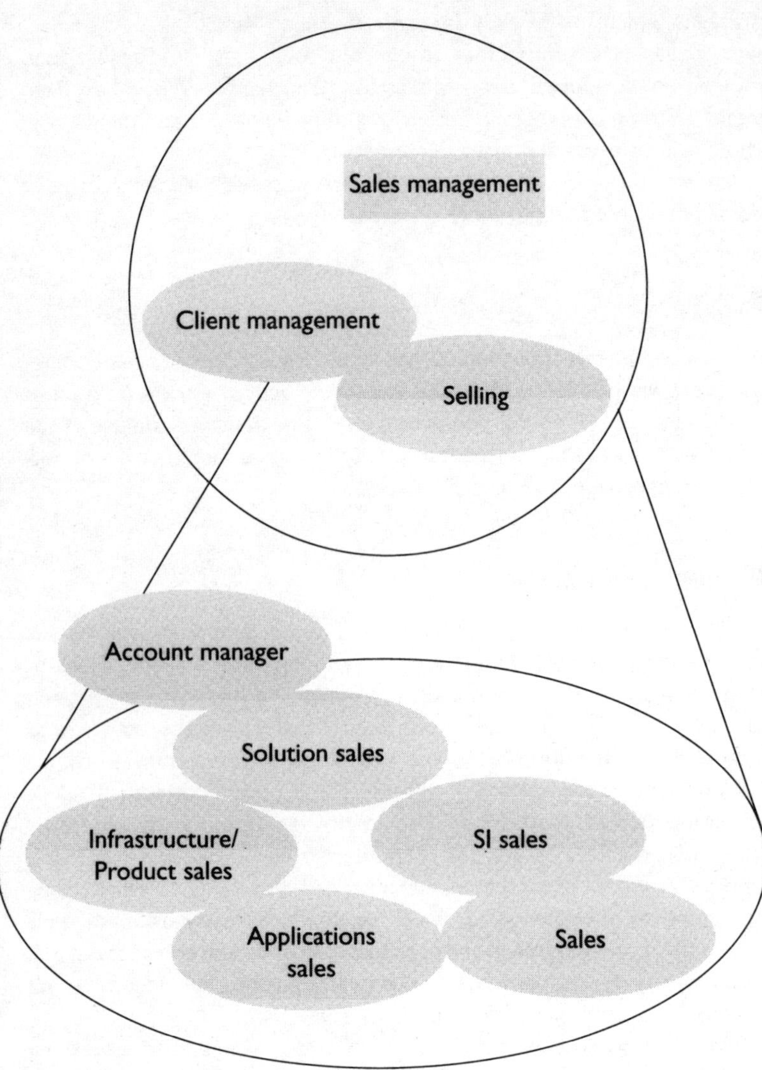

Figure 3.11 An example of an ICL 'Community'

ICL refer to their competencies as 'capabilities'. These are incorporated into role profiles which list accountabilities, performance indicators, technical/functional skills and capabilities required to achieve a role 'key purpose'. The capabilities were developed through consultation and participation of project teams, working teams, structured interviews and questionnaires. An example of the capabilities is included in Figure 3.12.

BUILDING RELATIONSHIPS	
HOW 1. Establishing trust and integrity in the relationship. 2. Establishing a mutual exchange of information. 3. Working with the customer as equal partners. 4. Networking at all levels in the client organisation and internally. 5. Maintaining and building relationships over time, despite setbacks or difficulties.	TO ACHIEVE ● To encourage greater openness and faith in ICL's proposals; to ensure a professional service. ● To ensure there are no surprises for ICL or the customer and establish an ongoing dialogue. ● To ensure s/he is up to date and aware of what is going on and can ensure the ICL is in the best position to deal with events. ● To ensure an ongoing relationship with the customer and see long term benefits.
COMMERCIAL AWARENESS	
HOW 1. Understanding the economics of the business. 2. Understanding the legal, commercial and financial impact of actions/decisions.	TO ACHIEVE ● To assess the ongoing benefit to ICL of the sale (eg. marginal costs, transfer costs, product margins). ● To create value of the customer at the right margin with the least risk.
COMMUNICATING AND PERSUADING	
HOW 1. Checking own understanding; questioning and probing to establish information. 2. Asking direct and/or difficult questions. 3. Interpreting what is not said as well as what is communicated; 'reading between the lines'. 4. Presenting information in a way which both clarifies and sells the ideas/proposed actions. 5. Negotiating to establish an acceptable solution and achieve 'win:win'.	TO ACHIEVE ● to ensure full understanding, to get to the real issues and establish key facts. ● to ensure the difficult issues are addressed rather than avoided. ● to understand the customer's unspoken concerns and feelings and address these appropriately, putting the customer at ease. ● to help colleagues from different disciplines understand the customer's issues. ● to gain buy-in from internal colleagues; to gain the customer's commitment. ● to find compromises which achieve the optimum solution for ICL and add value for the customer.

Figure 3.12 ICL's sales professional community – capability definitions 1996

KNOWLEDGE OF ICL AND 3RD PARTY CAPABILITIES	
HOW 1. Knowing the strengths and weaknesses of ICL products; understanding what ICL can/cannot do. 2. Understanding other approved products and maintaining an awareness of other comparable products which are available.	TO ACHIEVE ● To assess what is technically possible. ● To marry business needs with complex technical requirements, matching them to the best solution.
PLANNING, MONITORING & FORECASTING	
HOW 1. Using available tools to help with operational planning process; scheduling activities. 2. Establishing personal action plans by breaking targets into tactical steps and prioritising; monitoring and replanning over time. 3. Forecasting for coming years, taking a strategic focus.	TO ACHIEVE ● To identify who, what, why, when and plan accordingly (Blue Sheet). ● To identify specific customers to focus on to achieve an agreed sales target; to qualify the return on effort (time, resources). ● To keep the funnel full; to have a long term sales and relationship management strategy.
LEADERSHIP	
HOW 1. Clarifying what's to be done; allocating work and responsibility to others; keeping momentum going. 2. Pulling people from diverse backgrounds with differing expertise into a united team with common goals; demonstrating own enthusiasm and commitment to the objective.	TO ACHIEVE ● To ensure tasks are achieved according to plan. ● To win commitment from internal and external resources; to manage the bid process to best effect.

Figure 3.12 (continued)

UNDERSTANDING THE CUSTOMER	
HOW 1. Understanding the roles and needs of the key contact(s) and the internal processes/procedures which impact on them. 2. Understanding the customer's work environment, internal politics, business objectives and strategy. 3. Understanding the customer's industry, key economic issues and their competitive environment.	TO ACHIEVE ● To identify 'personal wins' for the customer; to help the customer address possible internal blocks. ● To provide a solution which fits the business. ● To provide specialist industry expertise and guide the customer accordingly.
MARKET AND COMPETITOR KNOWLEDGE	
HOW 1. Being aware of key industry issues and knowing the key players in the market. 2. Keeping up to date with developments in the market; showing awareness of emerging players and strength/weaknesses of competitors' products. 3. Understanding the strategic implications of ICL actions and competitive developments; understanding the dynamics of the market.	TO ACHIEVE ● To maintain credibility with the customer. ● To place ICL services/products in the best light in relation to competitors; to give professional advice. ● To assess the impact of bidding for a specific piece of work/losing a bid and the messages to the market.
OPPORTUNISM AND INITIATIVE	
HOW 1. Finding improved ways to tackle standard situations. 2. Turning problems into opportunities; finding creative alternatives when there is no obvious way forward. 3. Generating high level ideas and conceptual approaches.	TO ACHIEVE ● To get in new contacts; to generate leads. ● To benefit both ICL and the customer; to ensure a sale can be achieved or to grow the sale. ● To ensure options aren't shut down too early; highlighting broad possibilities which others can test for proactivity.
EVALUATION AND JUDGEMENT	
HOW 1. Establishing the facts and hard data and making an objective assessment on the basis of this information. 2. Gathering a range of inputs to get the full picture, developing options/hypotheses and testing these out. 3. Taking a long term perspective and applying foresight and judgement to assess potential options.	TO ACHIEVE ● To identify target customers; to make basic 'go:no go' decisions. ● To ensure full understanding of the issues; to assess whether there is a real opportunity for ICL by checking assumptions with the customer. ● To balance short term gains with long term risk.

Figure 3.12

3.8 'IF YOU CAN'T MEASURE IT, YOU CAN'T MANAGE IT'

The following case study was first produced by Gary Ling of TMI, for one of my earlier books. It introduces work undertaken by a consortium of business organizations in respect of development and testing of 'change agent competences'.

The material in this study is a useful stimulus for thought.

This following case study shows how a set of change agent competencies has been developed by member organizations of the UK Learning Organization Network. The case study also illustrates three issues:

1. An initial networking process where generic competencies can be devised to suite the strategic human resource requirements of a broad range of commercial and non-commercial organizations.
2. How competence development can be driven by practical business requirements.
3. That competence development can be relatively inexpensive if driven by partner organizations which have a clear vision of what they are trying to achieve.

■ CASE STUDY ■

THE LEARNING ORGANIZATION NETWORK

The Learning Organization Network is an informal group of private and public sector organizations which have demonstrated their commitment to the concept of the learning organization. Member organizations include Rover, Digital Equipment, Midland Bank, Sainsburys, Time Manager International, Lucas, Rank Xerox, Milton Keynes College, the NHS and Royal Mail.

The group first met in London in November 1992, following an initiative from Rover, Digital Equipment and the RSA with support from the HRD Partnership. A second meeting was held in April 1993 at Rover where Barrie Oxtoby from the Rover Learning Business shared the work that Rover had done in developing a range of change agent competencies. Members of the group saw the value of this work and a team, coordinated by Ron Dillon, then training quality assurance manager at Rank Xerox, was formed to take it further.

The vision

The vision of the Network at this time was to devise a set of change agent competencies that:

- were relevant, credible and conceptually sound
- were sufficiently flexible to support the specific requirements of individual member companies
- recognized what people had already done
- potentially formed the basis of future development activity
- facilitated a self-assessment process that could be validated effectively and speedily
- allowed people who do not see themselves as change agents to recognize that they are.

Once the competencies had been developed, the role of the network was envisaged as being similar to that of an awarding body. In a less structured way than, for example, the awarding of NVQs, members nominated individuals within their organizations who they assessed as being change agents. In recognition of this, these individuals were then awarded certificates carrying the names and logos of all participating organizations.

Clearly, this vision was novel in its approach to the development of competencies. One team member described the way in which member organizations within the Learning Organization Network would work together in this process as a 'kind of change agent keiretsu'. It required the commitment of all concerned to the integrity of the process but since the essence of the change agent competencies is a recognition of continual individual and *organizational* learning, this was in keeping with the aims and objectives of the Learning Organization Network

The process

Rather than start with a blank sheet of paper, the team at the Rover Learning Business carried out an initial trawl of existing development work in the area of change management, before they embarked on devising their own set of change agent competencies. They contacted several professional bodies but found that the competency work currently underway appeared to be developed by 'systems professionals and lawyers who had little feeling for people'.

As a result, over a three month period, the Rover Learning Business

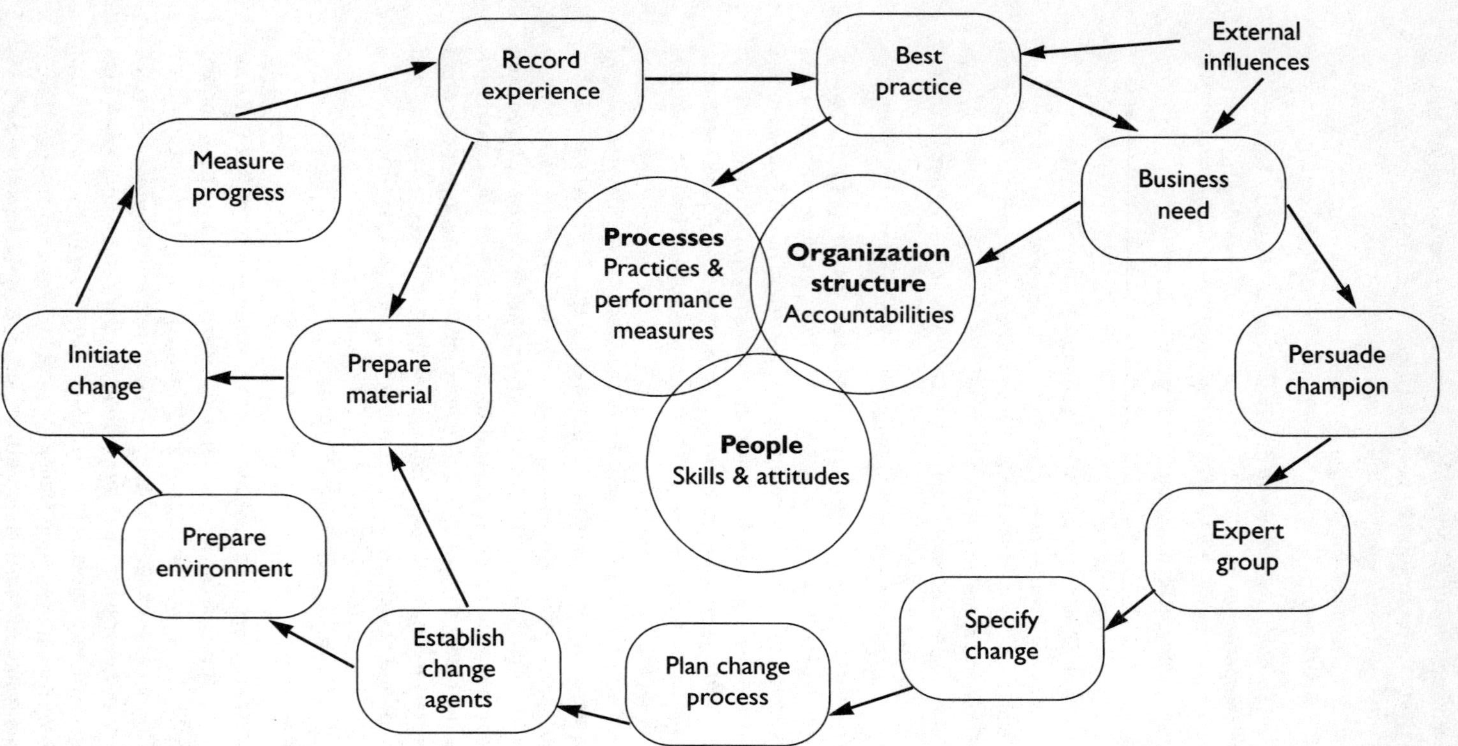

Figure 3.13 The change cycle

started work on its own set of change agent competencies for l within the Rover organization, linked closely to supporting the pany's business strategy. The key question addressed by this work 'What competencies do you need to make the learning process wo from a learning business viewpoint?' Initially, 82 competencies were developed in this way and tested internally with change agents within Rover.

In networking with other organizations interested in developments in this area, Rover came across the work of Peritas, the ICL company specializing in people and organizational development. Peritas had developed a practical approach to competencies that they were marketing externally as a commercial enterprise. It was the initial contributions of both these organizations that the team from the Learning Organization Network set to work on, and Peritas has now used the Rover framework to produce a model of change and change agent competencies for any business manager. The Learning Organization Network is now validating these competencies in a variety of business environments.

The framework

The 'change cycle' in Fig 3.13 outlines the model of change within which Peritas have developed this set of change agent competencies.

The change cycle illustrates the stages that change agents have to go through in order to bring about value-adding change. Changing processes, organizational structure and the skills and attitudes of people are the three areas which are specifically identified as the targets of change.

Clearly, change agents have to understand the external influences that affect both best practice and their organization's business needs. While many businesses will be affected by the same external influences, such as those which impact the economic environment generally, change agents will also be expected to appreciate factors that specifically impact their organizations.

From best practice and business needs the Learning Organization Network team has developed a set of competencies for each of the areas identified in the change cycle.

The future

Although still in its infancy, the process by which these competencies have been developed so far has generated some considerable interest in Europe, where at a recent meeting of the European Consortium for Learning Organizations, the UK's work in this area was recognized as being significantly further advanced than its continental partners. A study group has now been set up in Finland to change and develop these competencies further.

Meanwhile, while recognizing that these competencies are not cast in stone, organizations in the Learning Organization Network are soon to be invited to make a more tangible commitment to the competencies developed so far, by offering the use of their corporate logos on the first certificates issued to those individuals recognized as competent change agents.

— 4 —

The Competence Change Toolkit

You will need a notebook to work through this chapter, which provides a staged approach to the development and implementation of a competence framework as a tool for organizational change.

I do not propose that a competence framework is the ultimate solution to business problems – I do, however, suggest that its use in a flexible and creative way will facilitate action to instigate and manage a change programme.

I have incorporated examples of the revised UK management standards, developed by the Management Charter Initiative in 1997, into this chapter with permission from MCI and HMSO Licence. These nationally recognized standards of competence provide a starting point for consideration of management roles in the change process. The format of these standards conforms to the UK model of competence which underpins NVQs. They are, therefore, essentially outcome-based. However, 'personal' or 'behavioural' competences are referenced in context, making a more rounded product for use by organizations which wish to combine both occupational and behavioural descriptors in their competence framework.

The Competence Change Toolkit adopts an initial top-down approach, requiring clear direction and strategic management skills. Further stages require a consultative style, drawing on experience, ideas and creativity across and between all levels and divisions of an organization.

Future trends and requirements must be a keynote of the planning and development stages; in particular, there is little point in developing a framework which will be outdated before implementation has been completed.

How to use this toolkit

- **4.1 Mission culture and values**

  This section briefly reviews concepts and ideas on mission values and culture and provides guidelines on formulating working statements and models for incorporation into a competence framework. These three components of organizational effectiveness need to be reflected in a 'common language' that can be used to make them transparent and 'come alive' in everyday work activities. You will be asked to prepare some initial notes for later work on developing your framework.

- **4.2 Strategy**

  This section aims to stimulate ideas and review the role of strategic thinking within the organization. A checklist for use by those responsible for planning and implementing change is included. This section should be reviewed before beginning the work involved in later sections in order to clarify the strategic role of a competence framework.

- **4.3 Developing competences/ies**

  This section outlines approaches to the development of competences that will result in a framework for change. Pitfalls are identified.

- **4.4 Planning structure**

  The use of a competence framework in restructuring effective operations is reviewed and ideas explored.

- **4.5 Profile Roles**

  Preparing for the future depends on having the right people in the right place *all* the time. This demands flexibility in role profiling. This section explores how this can be established.

- **4.6 Review the HR functions**

  The potential for competence-based performance management depends on its effective and efficient use across the HR function. This section explores ideas and practical applications.

Evaluate and review

Completing the feedback loop is essential. Evaluation measures will be built into the system at all levels, building an efficient monitoring and planning structure and thus increasing flexibility and response of an organization to a constantly changing market. The competence framework, if used to its full potential, allows restructuring to take place to meet immediate and/or long term needs.

Figure 4.1 illustrates the change model. Figure 4.2 illustrates the resulting integrated performance management system. On page 118 you will find a 'Dictionary for Organizational Change' which, I hope, will help you through the remainder of this chapter.

The research and development work required to establish and implement this model is extensive and requires top-down commitment. Issues relating to obtaining this commitment are explored in this and previous chapters.

This book can provide an overview and some practical aids for assisting with this work, but the ideas and techniques should be adapted to meet the needs of each organization. Careful preparation will result in a better quality and more user-friendly product – but remember to maintain a healthy dialogue and interaction between planning and action! You will not find all the answers in one planning session. Be thorough but creative; review regularly and gather information and feedback from all sources. Focus on making the management of performance 'come alive', along with values and customer excellence. I have included an extensive reference section to enable you to explore concepts and ideas.

The Competence Change Model

There are six stages to this model, which aims to translate the vision/mission/values into action through a competence framework; see Figure 4.1.

Integrated Performance Management

Establishing a competence framework sets in place key components of performance management, a 'common language' for HR functions. Combined with information technology this provides a powerful, effective and efficient system; see Figure 4.2.

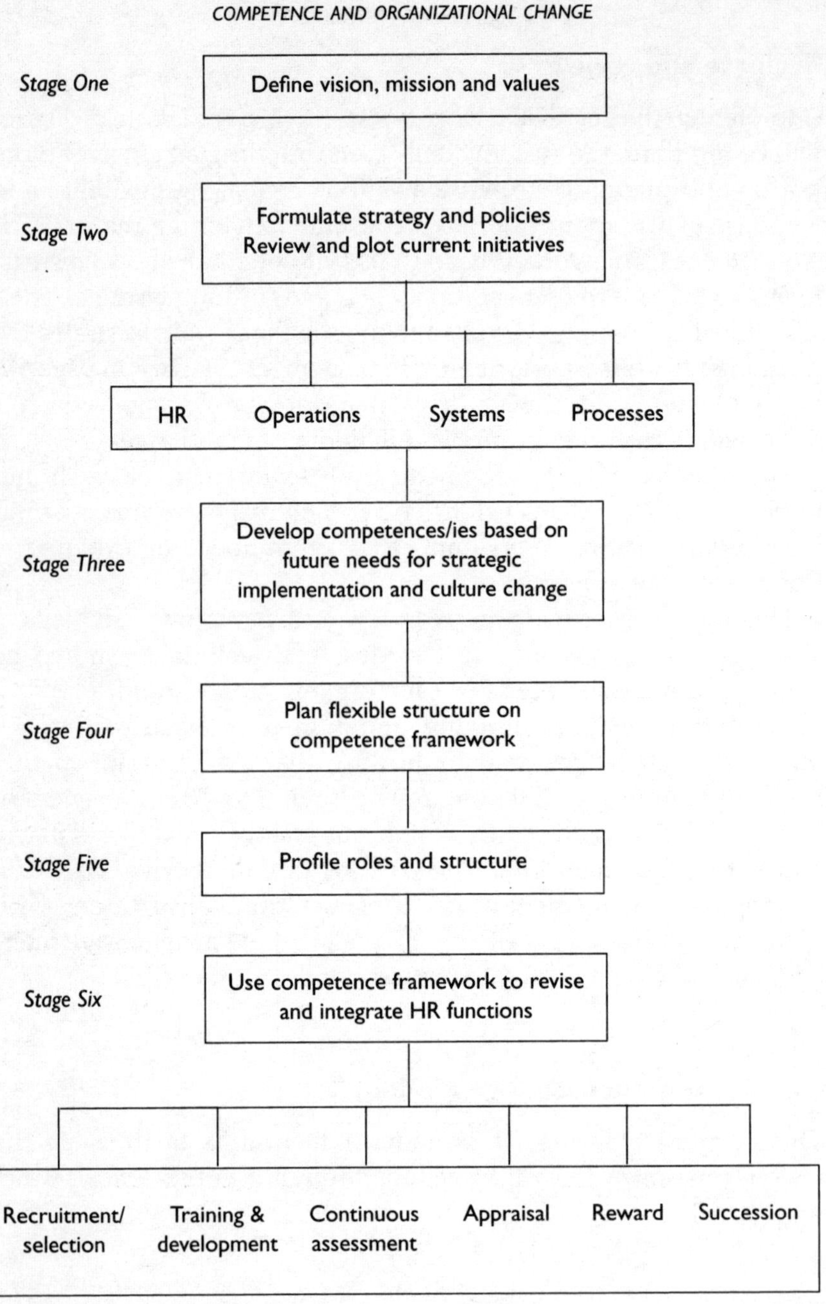

Figure 4.1 The competence change model

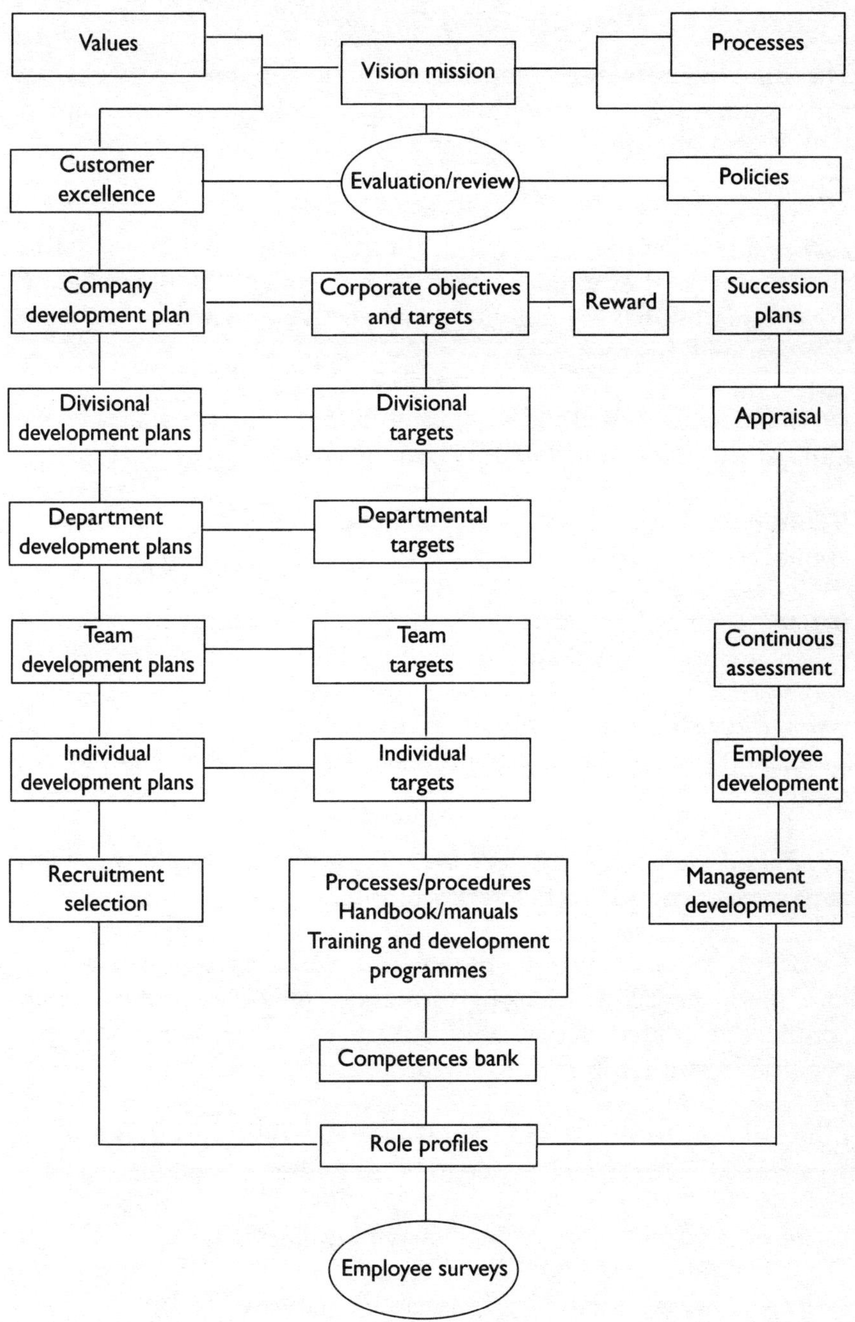

Figure 4.2 Integrated performance management – operational system

Dictionary for Organizational Change

The following terms are frequently found in common use in change programmes. The given definitions may be helpful (extract adapted with permission from *IRS Management Review*, January 1997, 1, 4, pp. 55–57).

Achievement centre An organizational culture that is geared to achieving a goal or an ideal that the members of the organization are also committed to attaining – irrespective of whether it is what the customer desires.

Attitudes Views that individuals hold that influence their behaviour. Attitudes are not stable and can be changed.

Behaviour The way a person acts. Behaviour is governed by situational contingencies.

Beliefs The information an individual has about an object – beliefs generally link the object to a specific attribute.

Change agents An individual or group of individuals who play a significant part in any change process – initiators, coordinators and facilitators.

Command and control culture Typically hierarchical, with employees closely directed and controlled.

Contingency management Based on the notion that every behaviour has a consequence – performance can be improved when people are offered a desirable outcome. People also know the penalties resulting from substandard performance.

Core values Essential and enduring organization guiding principles which have intrinsic value to those within an organization.

Corporate culture The 'official' way of doing things.

Culture audits Method of assessing culture and measuring progress of change programmes by asking employees' views.

Culture lag The degree to which an organization's culture lags behind needs.

Culture mapping A method of reviewing current cultural practices and their relation to intended cultural values.

Dysfunctional cultures Used by Peters and Waterman (1987) to relate to strong cultures that are not functioning well.

Empowerment A requirement for employees to take more responsibility for their actions and behaviours and to perform some of the decision-making functions.

Force field model (Kurt Lewin) A method for assessing an organization's disposition to change – identifies driving forces and restraining forces.

Harmonization A process to introduce the same benefits package to all employees – also called single status arrangements.

MBO Management by objectives – to achieve desired results, managers should define what needs to be done and review progress regularly.

Organizational culture The way things are *actually* done within an organization.

Performance management A process which integrates individual and organization objectives to achieve improvement in employee and corporate performance.

Power levers Operational strategies that can be used either separately or individually to exercise power.

Psychological contract 'The (unwritten) set of expectations operating at all times between every member of the organization and the various managers and others' (Schein, 1980).

Stakeholder analysis A means of identifying the different perspectives that organizational members will have of change initiatives.

Subculture Separate culture existing within the dominant culture.

Uncertainty avoidance The degree to which organizations tolerate deviance from the dominant norms and values.

4.1 DEFINE VISION, MISSION AND VALUES

> 'The Management that does not ask "What is our Mission?" when the company is successful is, in effect, smug, lazy and arrogant'.
>
> (Drucker, 1973)

Mission statements

Peter Drucker proposed four key questions in respect of formulating a mission statement:

- What is our business?
- Who is our customer?
- Where is our customer?
- What is our value to our customer?

Mission statements vary tremendously – as does the understanding or intention related to their creation. We are familiar, no doubt, with the short, sharp mission statement created for ease of use with employees and customers, for example Hertz's 'We try harder' or British Airways' 'Putting people first' or AT&T's 'Universal service'.

This type of mission statement serves its purpose in creating and maintaining awareness of key goals or values, but was probably derived from a longer and more detailed statement with a different purpose.

Mission and strategy need to be closely related and careful thought must therefore be given to formulating both. A mission or vision needs to define the business domain, or as Levitt (1960) states, 'the wider business'. The ethical domain is, today, equally as important. Other factors influence the formulation of mission statements, for example, profit, expansion plans, image, customer base.

When formulating a mission statement, or reviewing an existing one, it is helpful to consider the target audience. Is this statement to be used to:

- Motivate employees?
- Present a positive image to customers?
- Promote the organization?
- Help formulate a strategy?
- Redefine values?

- Redefine culture?
- Redefine goals?
- Lead diversification?
- Lead change in the core business?
- Redefine customers?
- Any combination of the above?

Campbell and Tawadey (1990) of Ashridge Management College suggest that 'a sense of mission is essentially an emotional feeling by the people in the organization... An organisation with a sense of mission has captured the emotional support of its people'. This would seem to be an essential component of a mission statement. There is a little point in defining a mission or goal unless energy and commitment can be harnessed to achieve it.

Ashridge has developed its own 'mission model', outlined in Campbell and Yeung (1991), that has four components, represented as a diamond:

- *purpose* – why the company exists
- *strategy* – its commercial rationale
- *values* – what senior management believe in
- *standards and behaviour* – policies and behaviour (patterns that guide how the company operates).

Note that 'standards' in this model relate to 'policies' and not to expectations of performance such as those defined in competences. Terminology can be confusing, especially when 'competences' and 'standards' are often used interchangeably.

Tom Peters (1988) refers to 'visions', again a term often interchangeable with 'mission'. He suggests that 'Visions are aesthetic and moral, as well as strategically sound ... Developing a vision and values is a messy, artistic process'. He cites examples of posters and cards which declare vision and values and suggests that these may be helpful, but only when the mission and values are 'lived convincingly'. He proposes eight key components of effective visions:

1. Inspiring.
2. Clear, challenging and about excellence.
3. Make sense in the marketplace.
4. Stable but constantly challenged.
5. Beacons and controls.

6. Aimed at empowering our own people first, customers second.
7. Prepare for the future, but honour the past.
8. Lived in details, not broad stokes.

He also adds that effective visions should:

- stress flexibility and execution
- stand the test of time.

This is quite a tall order. Perhaps you would like to test your own organization's mission/vision against these measures of effectiveness, using the following checklist.

MISSION STATEMENT CHECKLIST

Do you know your company's mission statement? ☐

Do other employees know the company's mission statement? ☐

In what ways is this mission actioned? Give three examples:

1. ....

2. ....

3. ....

Are your customers aware of the mission statement?

Is your mission statement:

Inspiring?	☐	Used as a control?	☐
Clear?	☐	Lived in detail?	☐
Challenging?	☐	Empowering to employees?	☐
Stable?	☐	Ready for the future?	☐
Constantly Challenged?	☐	Honouring the past?	☐

Mission and competence

If a mission defines the key purpose of an organization, it must be prepared in a way which lends itself to measurement – how else will we know if and when the mission is achieved?

If a mission reflects values and leads action, then a competence framework must reflect those same values and define expectations of the relevant action – action that will result in targets being met and customer excellence being consistently achieved.

Defining a competence framework is an opportunity to produce a tool which can help the organization's mission and values to 'live' in everyday work activity. In order to clarify this for yourself, consider the following key questions:

- What key values are explicit?
- What key values are implicit?
- What key behaviours are explicit?
- What key behaviours are implicit?
- What customer expectations are explicit?
- What customer expectations are implicit?

Note your answers for use in preparing your competence framework.

Further useful advice and a critique of mission statements and their formulation and/or value can be found in *Creating a Sense of Mission* (Campbell and Yeung, 1991).

A final comment from Charles Handy, which appeared in *Management Today*, October 1996, p 35:

> 'There is nothing more exciting than losing oneself in a cause that is bigger than oneself, something that makes self-denial worthwhile and where success is shared, not hugged to oneself in secret.'

4.2 FORMULATE STRATEGY AND POLICIES

- What are the organization's objectives and goals?
- Should it seek to diversify, and if so, in what areas?
- How should it develop and exploit its current marketing position?

Ansoff, H I (1987)

Introduction

These three questions were presented by Ansoff as the key to forming an effective strategy. In his 1987 edition of *Corporate Strategy*, he presents an analysis of the interaction of strategic decision-making with that in the operational and administrative domains.

For those who are interested in reading a wealth of ideas on strategic thinking and planning a good starting point may be the library section on World War II, for this is where must of the initial conceptual work can be found. The ideas generated here were adopted and adapted by leading lights such as Robert McNamara, who became US Secretary of Defense under President John F Kennedy.

J von Neumann and O Morgenstern (1953) formulated a business-based strategic model that proposed methods of resolving conflict. This included two interpretations of strategy:

- *pure strategy* – a move, or series of moves in a specific area such as product development
- *grand strategy* – a statistical rule by which an organization can decide what pure strategy it should adopt in any given situation.

In 1962, the Harvard Business School published *Strategy and Structure* (Chandler, 1962). This provided a convincing argument that the structure of an organization is determined by its strategic goals and the resources employed to achieve them. This work has had a considerable long-term effect on many organizations in which the argument has been positively implemented on the basis that if strategic goals lead structure, then the function of an organization is 'to implement strategy'.

Perhaps the most influential writer on strategy and strategic thinking has been Ansoff. His earlier work, in the 1960s, provided a series of checklists and processes for strategic decision making. However, Ansoff himself later wrote that he thought his original approach was too prescriptive and lacked flexibility.

His book *Corporate Strategy* proposed that strategic decisions are often made within a 'restricting framework of resources' and are therefore limited to a choice of alternatives. He published a revised 'strategic success formula'. In this model he suggested that both internal and external capabilities should be matched to the 'turbulence of the business environment' (Ansoff, 1984).

Since Ansoff's work there have been many definitions and techniques relating to strategy and strategic thinking. For example:

> 'Corporate Strategy is an organization process, in many ways inseparable from the structure, behaviour and culture of the organization.'
>
> There are four components of strategy
>
> - market opportunity
> - corporate competence and resources
> - personal values and obligations
> - acknowledged obligations to people in society other than shareholders.
>
> Andrews, in Moore, J I (1992)

> 'Process of strategy formulation results in no immediate action. Rather, it sets the general direction in which the firm's position will grow and develop.'
>
> Ansoff (1984)

> 'The strategist's weapons are strategic thinking, consistency and coherence… no dramatic leap or stroke of genius is involved… the strategist's method is very simply to challenge the prevailing assumptions with a single question – why?'
>
> Kenichi Ohmae (1983)

'Without driving forces there is no way to begin thinking through a scenario… some driving forces are critical… others don't require much attention. Whenever I look for driving forces, I first run through a familiar litany of categories:

- society
- technology
- economics
- politics
- environment.'

Schwartz (1991)

> 'To manage strategy is in the first place to manage stability, not change. Indeed, most of the time, senior managers should not be forming strategy at all, they should be getting on with making their organisations as effective as possible in pursuing the strategies they already have... To manage strategy is not so much to promote change as to know when to do so.'

Mintzberg (1989)

> 'a firm gains competitive advantage by performing strategically important activities more cheaply and better than its competitors... Differences among competitor "value chains"* are a key source of competitive advantage.'

Defining strategy

Confused? Perhaps the one thing that becomes clear when reading texts on strategy or strategic thinking is that there is no clear and common definition! At times, one cannot be sure whether the topic under discussion is strategy, competitive strategy, business strategy, or strategic management.

I find it easier to relate particular authors to particular subjects in this respect. For example:

Porter, Michael (1985)	competitive advantage
Andrews, K (in Moore, J, 1992)	corporate strategy strategic management business strategy
Mintzberg Henry (1994)	strategic management
Ansoff, H I (1984)	strategic management
Ohmae, Kenidi (1983)	competitive strategy business strategy

* The 'value chain' is a concept by which every single activity within the cycle of production, marketing, delivery and support can be broken down and its interaction with others identified.

Porter (1985)

Using these authors as a guide, I can prepare my own working view of 'strategy':

- *competitive advantage and competitive strategy*
  - producing a checklist for profiling competitors
  - creating value for customers

- *corporate strategy*
  - the pattern of decisions in an organization that determines and reveals its objectives, purposes or goals, produces principal policies and plans for achieving goals
- *business strategy*
  - how a company positions itself in a given business
  - there are three main players: the corporation, the customer and the competition.

These may be rather simplified descriptors but they serve as a useful working tool in what can become a complex and value-laden debate in the board room.

Strategy and competence

When thinking of a competence framework as a tool for change, its strategic value must be considered. Anyone with responsibility for managing change and/or developing a competence framework should therefore have, at minimum, a working knowledge of corporate and business strategies.

This is of particular importance if the competence framework is to include 'core', 'corporate' or 'strategic' competences, ie measures of the organization's performance. These high level measures should reflect strategies (as well as desired culture and values).

The following checklist should prove helpful in determining your level of understanding of your organization's strategy and in stimulating ideas for your development of a competence framework. This checklist incorporates key questions identified by Andrews (quoted in Moore, 1992) and extends these to incorporate the component of competence.

STRATEGY CHECKLIST

1. Check your understanding of your organization's strategy

A) Has the strategy been made clear – in words or practice?
B) Is the strategy consistent with the personal values and aspirations of key managers?
C) Does the strategy present a stimulus for effort and achievement?
D) Does the strategy present a common goal(s)?
E) Where does the strategy position your organization?
F) What aspects of the organization require change if strategic goals are to be achieved?
G) Is the strategy translated into objectives for lower management levels?
H) Does the strategy address customers, competitors and the corporation?
I) Does the strategy match the needs of the defined market?

2. Check the needs of your proposed competence framework

A) Is the strategy consistent with corporate competence and resources?
B) Do you need to define 'strategic competences' (organization competence)?
C) Are there new competences to be incorporated?
D) How will values be incorporated?
E) Has 'competence' been defined and agreed?

Review and plot current initiatives

Most organizations undertake more new initiatives than any one person in that organization is aware of. These all cost time, money and effort. They frequently have overlapping or even duplicating or conflicting objectives.

Plot the objectives and progress of initiatives and projects in your organization. Explore details of each one in terms of:

- title of project
- project manager
- objectives
- resources allocated – finance, people, equipment

- progress against milestones
- duration
- end product
- relationship to other initiatives
- contribution to strategy.

Once you have completed this review consider where the duplication or conflict occurs. What are the implications of this duplication/conflict? What are the costs involved? What action can be taken to avoid continuance of this situation?

Often, the use of a competence framework (and early stages of this probably exist somewhere in this mound of initiatives) can help to draw these projects together, providing the missing 'glue' for all these disparate pieces of development.

4.3 DEVELOPING COMPETENCES/IES FOR STRATEGIC IMPLEMENTATION AND CULTURE CHANGE

Introduction

Various examples of competence frameworks are illustrated in the case studies in Chapter 3. For example, ICL and Air UK studies provide illustrations of behaviourally-based frameworks. The MCL Group study of Mazda's experience refers to NVQ standards, but also incorporates behaviour-based and company-specific competence statements

Organization-led frameworks

The most effective frameworks are those which are developed through careful consideration of *what the organization needs for the future.*

Many competence developments start by asking 'What do people do?' or, 'How do people behave?' This can be a big mistake! Asking this question first results in answers which reflect individual perceptions of expectations, and reflect the status quo.

An effective competence framework is

- business-led
- future focused
- measurable
- fit for purpose

This can be best achieved by starting with the question: 'What does the organization need for future success?'

Use of the best tools for analysis can then reveal the key components of competence; see Figure 4.4.

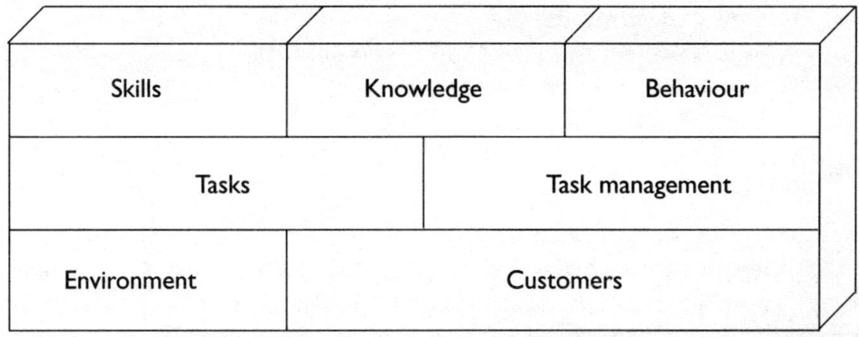

Figure 4.4 Components of competence

This approach avoids the emphasis on any one component and takes a broad view of competence.

Commitment

A consultative approach engenders involvement and commitment, whether through workshops, structured interviews or project groups. This commitment and 'buy-in' is critical to success, as evidenced in all the case studies included in Chapter 3. As the ICL case study highlights, top-down commitment and communication makes for easier development and implementation – but is not always possible. A second option is the identification of a champion.

Communication

The next key issue is communication. Involvement of all employees must be generated through the provision of information. A company-wide briefing is a valuable means of informing, motivating and surveying the current picture.

The critical communication should let everyone know:

- what is going to be developed
- why
- how employees can be involved
- what benefits will accrue for
  - the organization
  - individuals

- when developments will start
- who has project management responsibility
- who is the project champion.

Planning

This implies that a degree of planning has been undertaken in order that the questions above can be anticipated within an initial briefing. The checklists included in earlier sections of this chapter will have assisted with this planning. Critical aspects to keep in mind are:

- clarify mission/values/culture
- prepare strategy to achieve mission
- agree meaning and purpose(s) of proposed competence framework
- identify/plot current initiatives and their contribution to strategy.

If these early discussions have taken place, you will be ready to plan the development process and to communicate this to all employees.

Dialogue between planning and action

One word of caution at this point. There is a dangerous plateau reached by many organizations during the planning stage. This occurs when an acceptable level of uncertainty has yet to be defined.

The planning process will produce one thing only – a plan. *Action* is required to take this forward. This may sound obvious, but consider how often you have attended planning meetings, and agreed a 'plan' only to find that no action follows. This may well be due to uncertainty about outcomes – a need to 'have the answers' before taking real action.

An effective project requires a dialogue between action and planning. This means that the answers are not clear at the beginning of action – if they were, you probably would not need to take the action!

Developing competences/ies is a project that needs to be undertaken in an environment of acceptable uncertainty. No one really knows what the competences/ies will look like, or how they will fit together until all the developmental issues have been explored. The development process is *iterative* (see Figure 4.5) – making a start with action is critical!

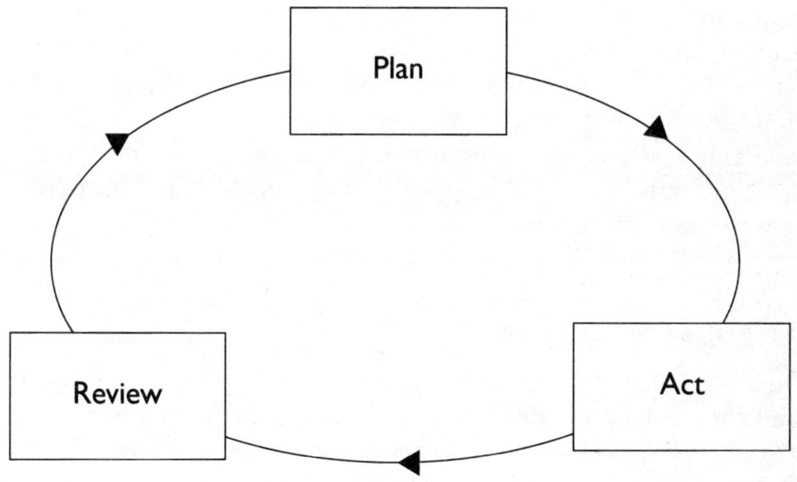

Figure 4.5 Dialogue between planning and action

Avoiding duplication of time and cost

I first introduced the concept of 'initiative overload' into my various presentations and conference papers in 1992, and included it in my book, *Integrating Quality and Competence* (Fletcher, 1993). It was always received with either a smile or nod of recognition. At some time, virtually everyone in an organization experiences 'initiative overload'! (See Figure 4.6.)

The duplication of time and cost involved can be considerable. It is therefore essential, at the preparation stage of competence development, to conduct a review of current and planned initiatives (see page 128).

A competence framework can act as the 'glue' which binds various initiatives into a cohesive, effective and 'living' performance management system. Initiatives relating to quality, procedures, customer service and many more all influence expectations of individual, team, department, division and organization performance and therefore need to operate within one systematic, user-friendly and accessible operation.

Selecting methods for development of competences/ies

If you have an agreed definition of competence (see page 39) and an agreed expectation of content and use (see page 130), your choice of development methods will be led by this agreement.

Outcome-based standards may be developed by a functionally-based or task-based approach. The level of detail to which such analysis by function is taken will also depend upon the agreed style of presentation, format and content.

Behaviourally-based standards may require techniques such as the behavioural event interview, repertory grids, behaviour-counting technique, structured interview or workshops.

Focus on business needs

Whatever type of competence you are developing, your starting point should be one of proactivity – what does the business *need*?

Your initial analysis will identify critical outcomes and/or behaviours for business success. Continuing levels of analysis will then have a good foundation for representing *future* needs. These levels of analysis should also relate to appropriate targets at divisional and departmental levels, which are themselves derived from organization targets, goals and objectives.

Use of measurement tools such as the balanced score card (see BUPA case study and page 71) and the performance pyramid (page 76) are increasingly to be found in organization developments.

Test and modify

The development of a competence framework is an iterative process requiring test and modification. An early consultative approach will set the groundwork for establishing and operating an efficient and effective feedback loop.

Aim for flexibility

If your preparation and planning has considered all influences and uses of a competence framework, flexibility will be inherent in the format, style and content of the developed competences/ies. If, however, your development has been led by one particular intended use, this will constrain and override the real potential.

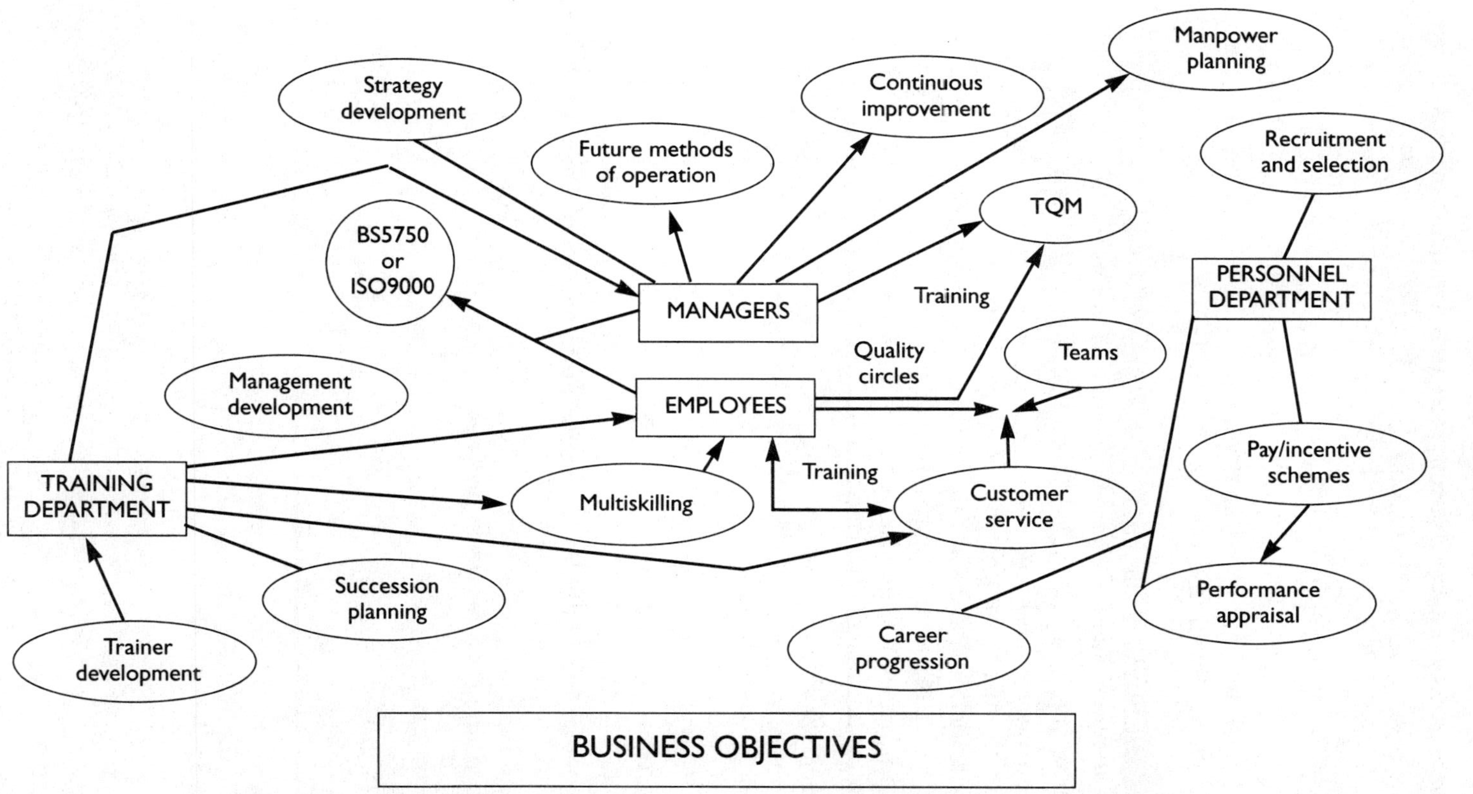

Figure 4.6 Initiative overload (Fletcher, 1993)

The next step will be profiling roles (the first stage of considering 'who' rather than 'what') and here flexibility will be essential. Restructuring on a minor and major scale may be required in the future and this needs to be undertaken within short time-scales. Transfer between roles and establishing project teams, promotion and succession planning can all be accomplished with minimal effort, if these uses of the framework are built in to the original plan.

A competence framework can be used for:

- restructuring a role
- assessing/measuring performance of individuals
- assessing/measuring performance of groups/teams
- improving work processes
- improving work procedures
- conducting a skills audit
- conducting a training needs analysis
- completing training design
- defining the current role requirements as a precursor to any of these activities
- defining the future role requirements as a precursor to any of these activities
- recruitment
- career development
- succession planning
- a new reward system
- identifying the mobility of employees across the organization
- conducting training evaluation
- linking internal assessment to external accreditation
- defining requirements for a new role or area of business.

4.4 PLAN STRUCTURE ON THE COMPETENCE FRAMEWORK

Realizing strategy through competent people

There is today a greater understanding and acceptance of the idea that people are the critical link between business strategy and business success.

Murray Dalziel (Hay/McBer, 1992) suggests that there are three main building blocks for change:

- *clarity* – knowing the direction in which you are going
- *commitment* – to make it happen
- *capability* – people with the required skills.

The term 'capability' is often used interchangeably with 'competence'; for example Sony BPE refer to their framework as 'capabilities'.

Role profiling

In his article on 'Building Competitive Advantage through People' (in Hay/McBer, 1992), Dalziel proposes that these three building blocks are linked with three ingredients of the human resources agenda, as illustrated in Figure 4.7. It is role design in particular that we are considering in this section.

Using a competence framework, roles can be 'profiled' to meet the needs of their particular function or purpose. Similar roles can be profiled and compared. Transferable competences/ies can be identified, allowing for greater mobility of employees.

Comparison of competencies across roles, between departments, through vertical progression or horizontal development yields valuable information for current and future use. The analysis can set the foundation for a new, flexible structure which can adapt to meet the demands of change caused by external and internal influences.

I have used both outcome-based competences and behavioural-based competencies to profile roles and often refer to this as 'role-mapping'. The concept is a simple one, as illustrated in Figure 4.8.

Using the UK system of NVQs, role profiling can be achieved through use of the unit-based structure. For example, the national standards for managers (Management Charter Initiative, 1997) comprise seven key areas of management activity, as outlined in section 4.5. Behavioural competencies can be used in the same way (see page 153).

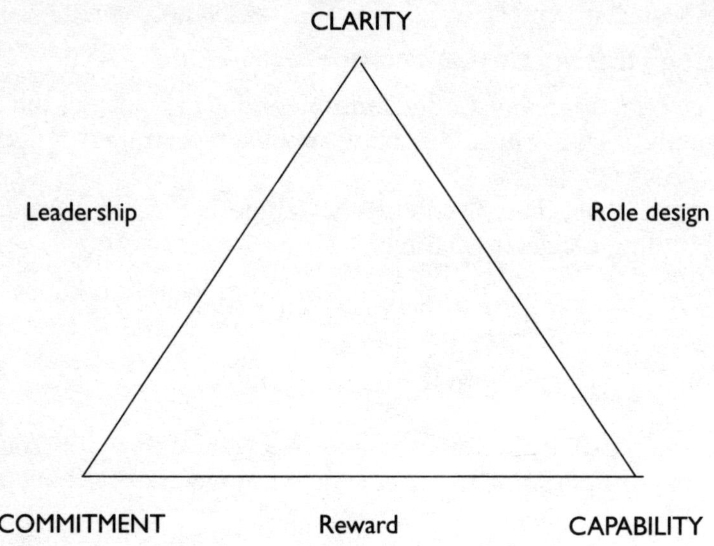

Figure 4.7 Linking the building blocks with the HR agenda (Dalziel, in Hay/McBer, 1992)

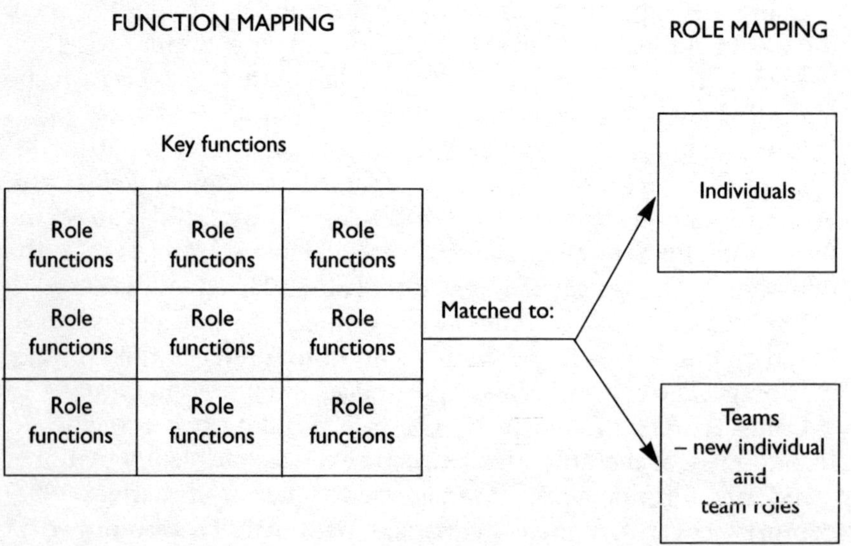

Figure 4.8 Role mapping

Competence and culture change

To establish roles and structure, the interaction between those roles must be considered. Role-holders are people – people interact both as role-holders and as individuals. Individuals have beliefs, behaviours and values – and these may conflict with those held, or intended, by the organization.

Culture change can only be achieved when a change occurs in the action people take. As previously explored, getting people behind a mission, goals or values is not merely a matter of issuing posters and publishing intent. People do not change simply because they have been *informed* of the change required. They change when they understand, believe in and act on the necessity for change.

Attitude surveys are useful tools for establishing a snapshot of the current culture (or multi-cultures in large organizations). Many organizations operate a 'customer satisfaction index' (CSI) for external customers. There is also an opportunity to assist and monitor culture change by establishing an internal CSI. Competence measures or indicators can be piloted with a programmed review schedule.

Several examples of the use of role profiling and of competence frameworks as the lead in structuring organizations are included in the case studies in Chapter 3. For example, ICL (page 101) has identified 'communities', while BUPA (page 71) works with 'functions'. Other companies may refer to 'families'.

4.5 PROFILE ROLES AND STRUCTURE

What does a role profile look like?

Profiles can take many forms. They should be designed to meet the needs of the organization and the purposes of the profiles themselves.

For example, a role profile may replace a number of job descriptions, see Figure 4.9. A profile may, in this example, represent a description of a 'family' of jobs. It therefore provides a generic reference point for a number of job titles, and can thus reduce the bureaucratic burden of the personnel department.

Both outcome-based and behavioural competences/ies can be used for profiling, if they are developed and designed for flexibility (see page 39).

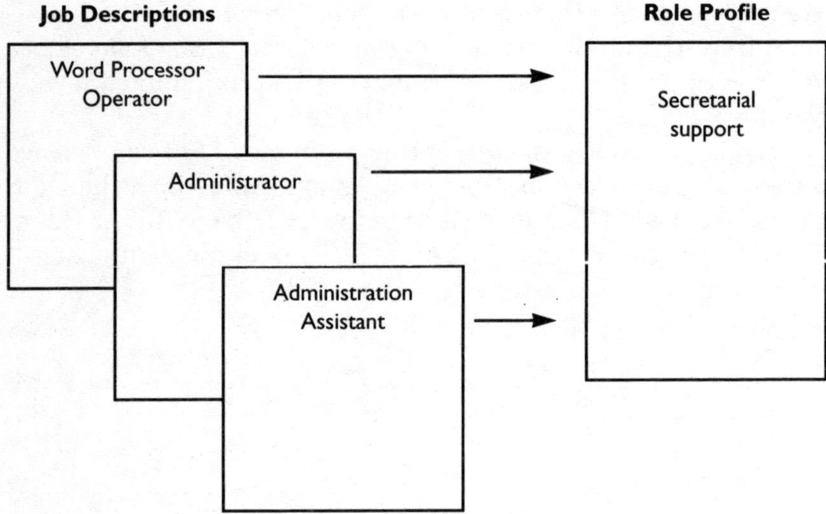

Figure 4.9 An example of a role profile

Using outcome-based standards

Figure 4.10 shows the revised structure of UK management standards produced by the Management Charter Initiative and launched in June 1997. It illustrates the 'integrated structure' of 'units of competence' under seven key topics (or families). These units are combined in different ways to form a national qualification structure.

3 = Level 3
4 = Level 4
5 (Ops) = Level 5 Operations
5 (Strategy) = Level 5 Stragetic
QM4 = Quality Management 4

MANAGE ACTIVITIES
Manage Activities describes the manager's work in managing the operation to meet customers' requirements and continuously improve its performance

Management Role	NVQ Level
A1 Maintain activities to meet requirements	**3**
A2 Manage activities to meet requirements	**4 QM4 (Optional)**
A3 Manage activities to meet customer requirements	**5 (Ops)**
A4 Contribute to improvements at work	**4**
A5 Manage change in organisational activities	**5 (Ops)**
A6 Review external and internal operating environments	**5 (Strategy)**
A7 Establish strategies to guide the work of your organisation	**5 (Strategy)**
A8 Evaluate and improve organisational performance	**5 (Strategy)**

MANAGE RESOURCES Manage Resources covers planning and using physical resources (money, premises, capital equipment, supplies and materials) effectively and efficiently.	
Management Role	**NVQ Level**
B1 Support the efficient use of resources	**3**
B2 Manage the use of physical resources (One must be in level 4)	**4 (Optional)**
B3 Manage the use of financial resources (One must be in level 4)	**4 (Optional)**
B4 Determine the effective use of resources	**5 (Ops)**
B5 Secure financial resources for your organisation's plans	**5 (Strategy) +** **5 (Ops) (Optional)**

MANAGE PEOPLE Manage People describes the work of managers in getting the most from their teams, allocating and evaluating work, and dealing with people problems. It also includes managing oneself and relations with others at work.	
Management Role	**NVQ Level**
C1 Manage yourself	**3**
C2 Develop your own resources	**4 + QM4**
C3 Enhance your own performance	**5 (Ops) +** **5 (Strategy)**
C4 Create effective working relationships	**3**
C5 Develop productive working relationships	**4 + QM4 (Optional)**
C6 Enhance productive working relationships	**5 (Strategy) +** **5 (Ops)**
C7 Contribute to the selection of personnel for activities	**3 (Optional)**

C8 Select personnel for activities	**4 (Optional) + 5 (Ops) (Optional)**
C9 Contribute to the development of teams and individuals	**3 (Optional)**
C10 Develop teams and individuals to enhance performance	**5 (Ops) (Optional) + 4 (Optional) + QM4 (Optional)**
C11 Develop management teams	**5 (Strategy)**
C12 Lead the work of teams and individuals to achieve their objectives	**3 (Optional)**
C13 Manage the performance of teams and individuals	**4 (Optional) + 5 (Ops) (Optional) + QM4 (Optional)**
C14 Delegate work to others	**5 (Strategy)**
C15 Respond to poor performance in your team	**4 (Optional) + 3 (Optional)**
C16 Deal with poor performance in your team	**5 (Ops) (Optional)**
C17 Redeploy personnel and make redundancies	**5 (Ops) (Optional)**

MANAGE INFORMATION Manage Information describes the manager's role in obtaining, analysing and using information effectively to take decisions. It also covers leading and contributing to meetings.	
Management Role	**NVQ Level**
D1 Manage information for action	**3**
D2 Facilitate meetings	**4 (Optional) + QM4 (Optional)**
D3 Chair and participate in meetings	**5 (Ops) (Optional) + 5 (Strategy)**
D4 Provide information to support decision making	**4 + QM4 (Optional)**
D5 Establish information management and communication systems	**5 (Ops) (Optional)**
D6 Use information to take critical decisions	**5 (Ops) + 5**

MANAGE ENERGY Manage Energy describes the role of those managers with special responsibility for ensuring the organisation develops and implements policies for using energy in the most efficient way.	
Management Role	**NVQ Level**
E1 Identify the scope of improvement in the way the organisation manages energy	**5 (Ops) (Optional)**
E2 Provide advice on the development and implementation of energy policies	
E3 Promote energy efficiency	**4 (Optional) + 5 (Ops) (Optional)**
E4 Monitor and evaluate energy efficiency	

E5 Identify improvements to energy efficiency	**3 (Optional) + 4 (Optional)**
E6 Provide advice and support for the development of energy efficient practices	**4 (Optional)**
E7 Provide advice and support for the development and implementation of systems to measure energy usage	
E8 Provide advice and support for improving energy efficiency	**4 (Optional)**

MANAGE QUALITY

Manage Quality describes the specialist role of the quality manager, covering total quality management, quality assurance and quality control.

Management Role	NVQ Level
F1 Promote the importance and benefits of quality	**5 (Ops) (Optional) + QM4 (Optional)**
F2 Provide advice and support for the development and implementation of quality policies	**4 (Optional) + QM4**
F3 Manage continuous quality improvement	**5 (Ops) (Optional) + QM4**
F4 Implement quality assurance systems	**4 (Optional) + QM4 + 5 (Ops) (Optional)**
F5 Provide advice and support for the development and implementation of quality systems	**QM4**
F6 Monitor compliance with quality systems	**4 (Optional) + QM4 + 5 (Ops) (Optional)**
F7 Carry out quality audits	**4 (Optional) + QM4 (Optional)**

MANAGE PROJECTS Manage Projects describes the role of those responsible for planning, controlling and completing projects to the sponsor's satisfaction.	
Management Role	**NVQ Level**
G1 Contribute to project planning and preparation	**4 (Optional)**
G2 Co-ordinate the running of projects	**4 (Optional)**
G3 Contribute to project closure	**4 (Optional)**
G4 Plan and prepare projects	**5 (Ops) (Optional)**
G5 Manage the running of projects	**5 (Ops) (Optional)**
G6 Complete projects	**5 (Ops) (Optional)**

Figure 4.10 NVQ levels referenced as standards published by the Management Charter Initiative 1997 (reproduced with permission of The Stationery Office).

The qualification structure contains standards that reflect the key competences required for a management role within an organization. The UK structure includes:

- Management Level 3
- Management Level 4
- Operational Management 5
- Strategic Management Level 5
- Quality Management Level 4
- Energy Management Level 4.

Each qualification may have mandatory and optional units, providing flexibility for individual companies and for individual managers. Figure 4.11 shows the unit structure for Operational Management Level 5. Each unit contains outcome-based standards, including performance criteria, evidence requirements, and references personal competencies, as illustrated in Figure 4.12.

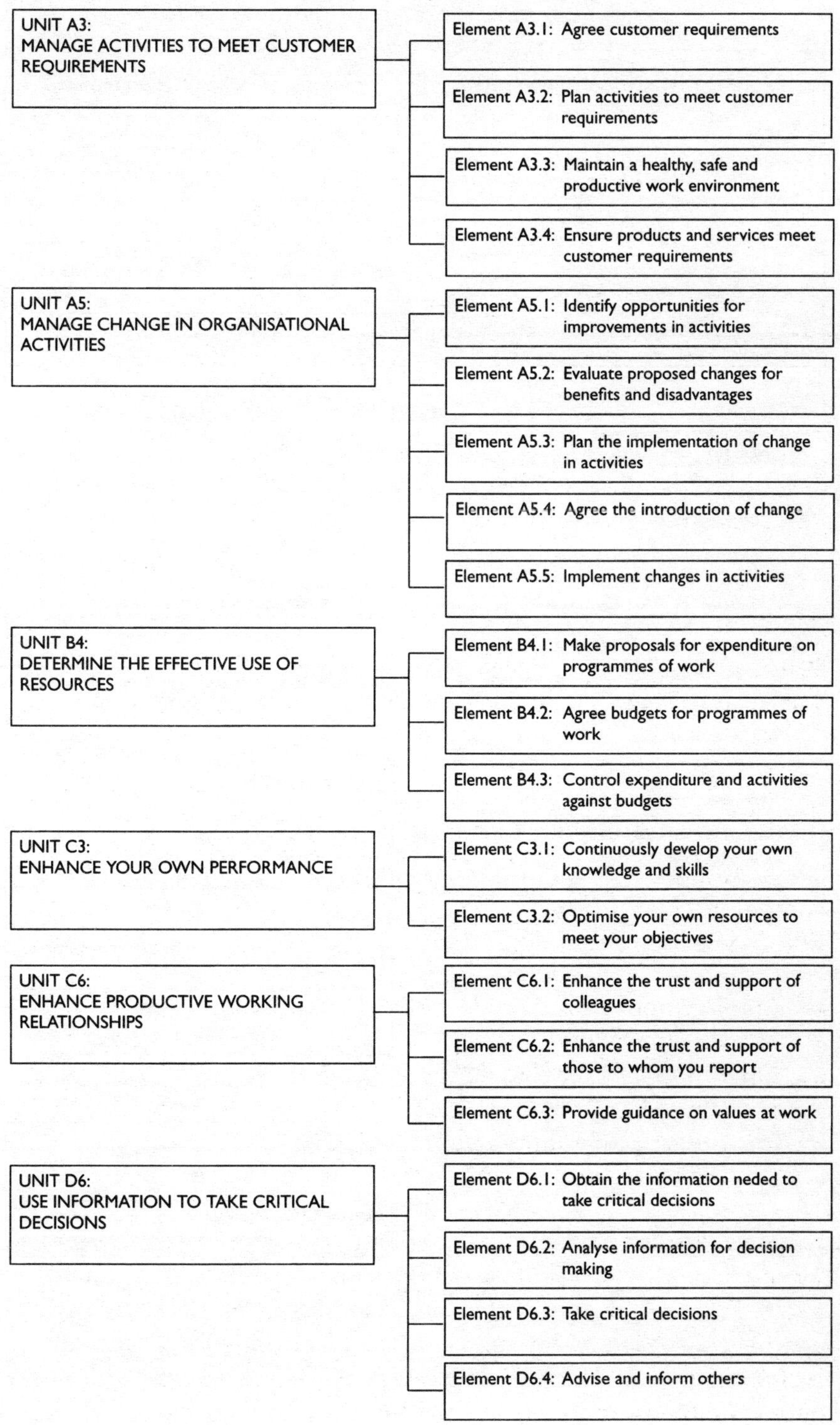
UNIT A3:
MANAGE ACTIVITIES TO MEET CUSTOMER REQUIREMENTS
Element A3.1: Agree customer requirements
Element A3.2: Plan activities to meet customer requirements
Element A3.3: Maintain a healthy, safe and productive work environment
Element A3.4: Ensure products and services meet customer requirements
UNIT A5:
MANAGE CHANGE IN ORGANISATIONAL ACTIVITIES
Element A5.1: Identify opportunities for improvements in activities
Element A5.2: Evaluate proposed changes for benefits and disadvantages
Element A5.3: Plan the implementation of change in activities
Element A5.4: Agree the introduction of change
Element A5.5: Implement changes in activities
UNIT B4:
DETERMINE THE EFFECTIVE USE OF RESOURCES
Element B4.1: Make proposals for expenditure on programmes of work
Element B4.2: Agree budgets for programmes of work
Element B4.3: Control expenditure and activities against budgets
UNIT C3:
ENHANCE YOUR OWN PERFORMANCE
Element C3.1: Continuously develop your own knowledge and skills
Element C3.2: Optimise your own resources to meet your objectives
UNIT C6:
ENHANCE PRODUCTIVE WORKING RELATIONSHIPS
Element C6.1: Enhance the trust and support of colleagues
Element C6.2: Enhance the trust and support of those to whom you report
Element C6.3: Provide guidance on values at work
UNIT D6:
USE INFORMATION TO TAKE CRITICAL DECISIONS
Element D6.1: Obtain the information neded to take critical decisions
Element D6.2: Analyse information for decision making
Element D6.3: Take critical decisions
Element D6.4: Advise and inform others

OPTIONAL UNITS (CHOOSE FOUR ADDITIONAL UNITS)

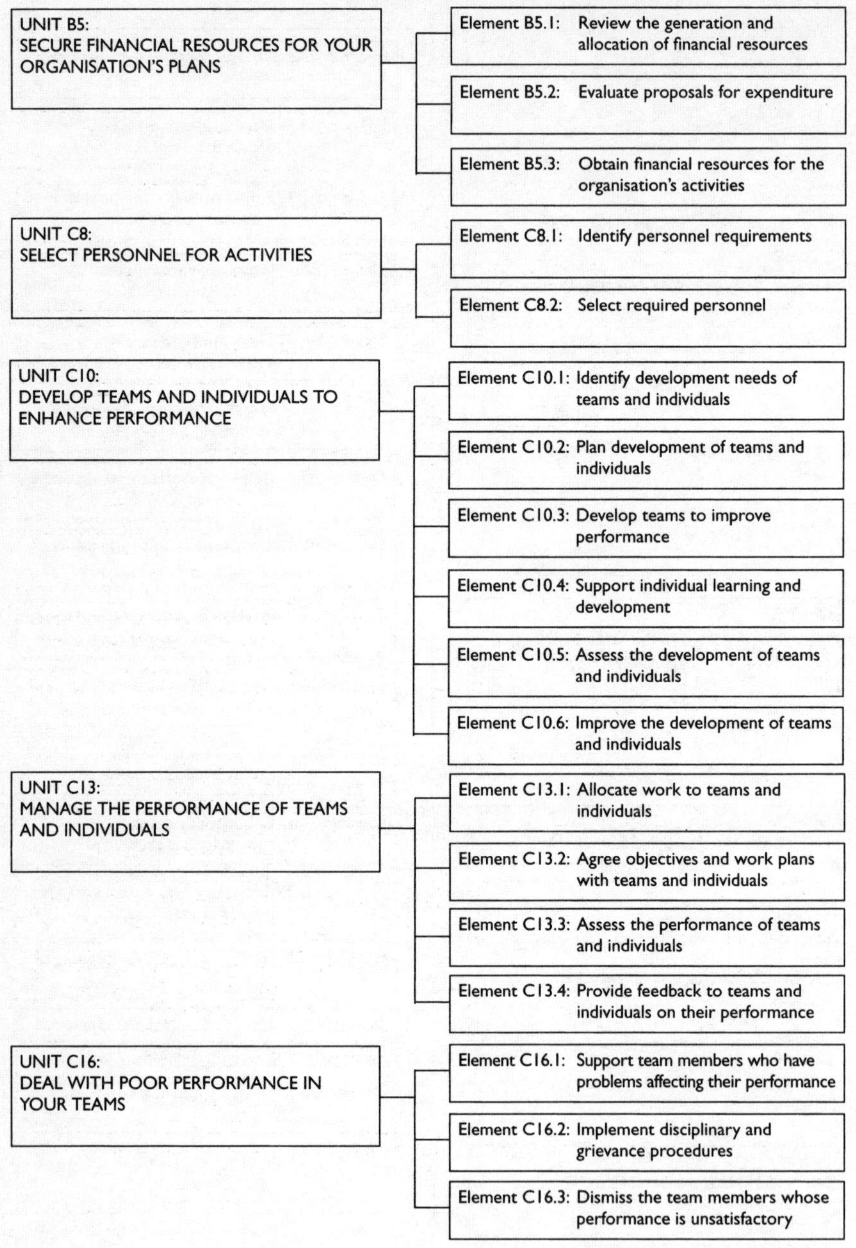
UNIT B5:
SECURE FINANCIAL RESOURCES FOR YOUR ORGANISATION'S PLANS
Element B5.1: Review the generation and allocation of financial resources
Element B5.2: Evaluate proposals for expenditure
Element B5.3: Obtain financial resources for the organisation's activities
UNIT C8:
SELECT PERSONNEL FOR ACTIVITIES
Element C8.1: Identify personnel requirements
Element C8.2: Select required personnel
UNIT C10:
DEVELOP TEAMS AND INDIVIDUALS TO ENHANCE PERFORMANCE
Element C10.1: Identify development needs of teams and individuals
Element C10.2: Plan development of teams and individuals
Element C10.3: Develop teams to improve performance
Element C10.4: Support individual learning and development
Element C10.5: Assess the development of teams and individuals
Element C10.6: Improve the development of teams and individuals
UNIT C13:
MANAGE THE PERFORMANCE OF TEAMS AND INDIVIDUALS
Element C13.1: Allocate work to teams and individuals
Element C13.2: Agree objectives and work plans with teams and individuals
Element C13.3: Assess the performance of teams and individuals
Element C13.4: Provide feedback to teams and individuals on their performance
UNIT C16:
DEAL WITH POOR PERFORMANCE IN YOUR TEAMS
Element C16.1: Support team members who have problems affecting their performance
Element C16.2: Implement disciplinary and grievance procedures
Element C16.3: Dismiss the team members whose performance is unsatisfactory

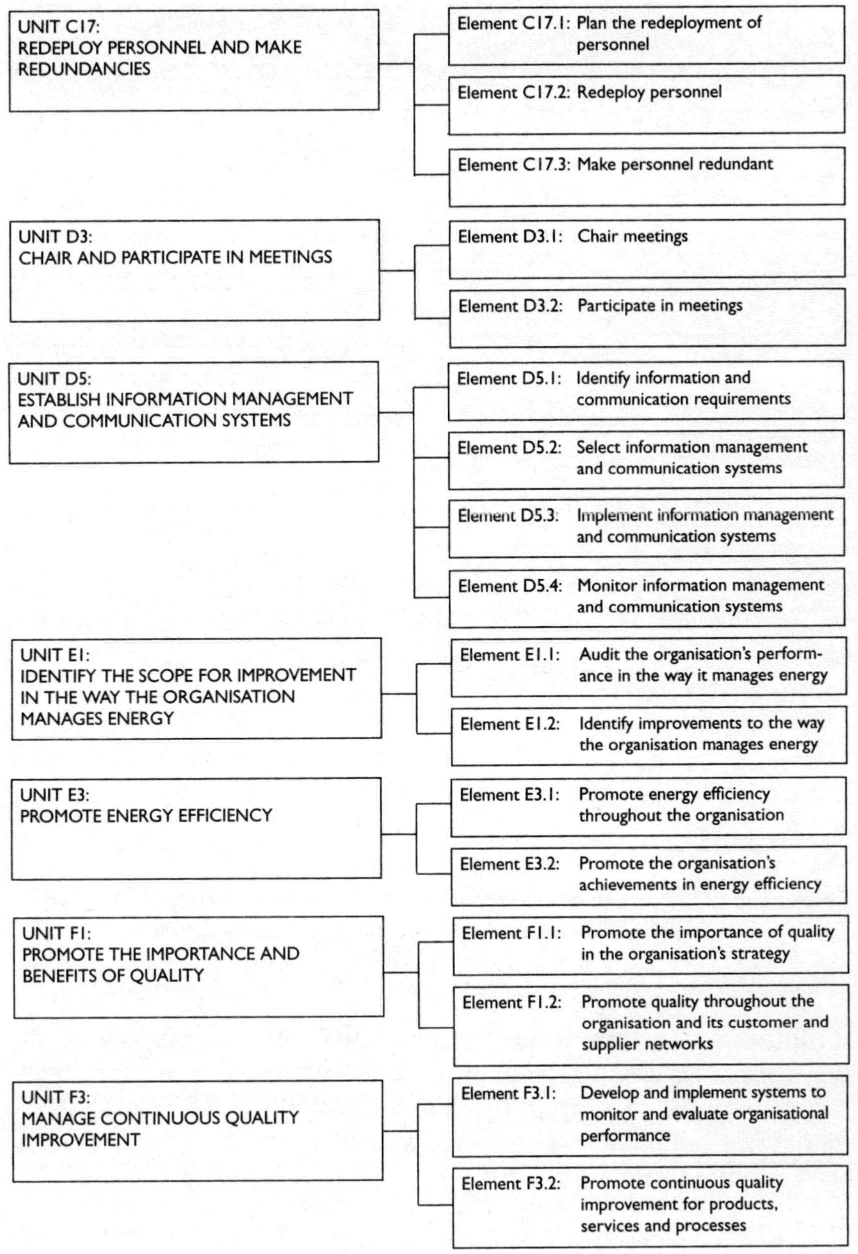
UNIT C17:
REDEPLOY PERSONNEL AND MAKE REDUNDANCIES
Element C17.1: Plan the redeployment of personnel
Element C17.2: Redeploy personnel
Element C17.3: Make personnel redundant
UNIT D3:
CHAIR AND PARTICIPATE IN MEETINGS
Element D3.1: Chair meetings
Element D3.2: Participate in meetings
UNIT D5:
ESTABLISH INFORMATION MANAGEMENT AND COMMUNICATION SYSTEMS
Element D5.1: Identify information and communication requirements
Element D5.2: Select information management and communication systems
Element D5.3: Implement information management and communication systems
Element D5.4: Monitor information management and communication systems
UNIT E1:
IDENTIFY THE SCOPE FOR IMPROVEMENT IN THE WAY THE ORGANISATION MANAGES ENERGY
Element E1.1: Audit the organisation's performance in the way it manages energy
Element E1.2: Identify improvements to the way the organisation manages energy
UNIT E3:
PROMOTE ENERGY EFFICIENCY
Element E3.1: Promote energy efficiency throughout the organisation
Element E3.2: Promote the organisation's achievements in energy efficiency
UNIT F1:
PROMOTE THE IMPORTANCE AND BENEFITS OF QUALITY
Element F1.1: Promote the importance of quality in the organisation's strategy
Element F1.2: Promote quality throughout the organisation and its customer and supplier networks
UNIT F3:
MANAGE CONTINUOUS QUALITY IMPROVEMENT
Element F3.1: Develop and implement systems to monitor and evaluate organisational performance
Element F3.2: Promote continuous quality improvement for products, services and processes

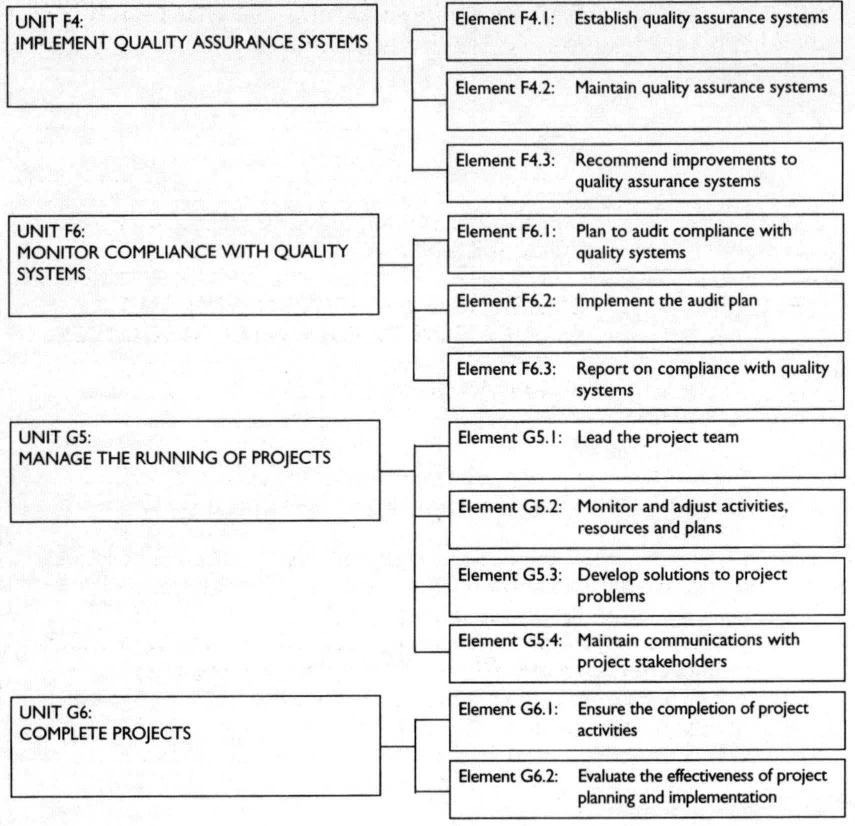

Figure 4.11 Structure of unit/elements for Operational Management Level 5 (reproduced with permission of The Stationery Office)

Profiling using these types of standards involves interviews or workshops to identify relevant units/elements. This is more than a 'job analysis'. A simple checklist for individuals to identify relevant units/elements will not suffice.

A profiling tool should consider:

- Which competences are relevant to the job/role?
- What is the appropriate level?
- What *evidence* exists to demonstrate the relevance of this competence (or should exist for a future, planned role)?
- How does this competence contribute to business objectives?

This last question is very important. There is a little point in profiling (and then assessing) competence if its contribution (and that of individuals and teams) is not linked to improvement in business performance.

UNIT TITLE: B5 SECURE FINANCIAL RESOURCES FOR YOUR ORGANISATION'S PLANS

ELEMENT TITLE: B5.1 REVIEW THE GENERATION AND ALLOCATION OF FINANCIAL RESOURCES

PERFORMANCE CRITERIA

You must ensure that

a) your systems for reviewing the **generation and allocation of financial resources** provide accurate, comprehensive and up-to-date information
b) the criteria you use for assessing the organisation's performance in the **generation and allocation of financial resources** takes account of the type of organisation, its context and culture
c) the criteria you use include commonly accepted performance measures for the **generation and allocation of financial resources**
d) your review shows how well the organisation is performing compared with other organisations
e) your review shows how effective the organisation's methods are compared to alternative methods of **generation and allocation of financial resources**
f) you gather, store and use information on the **generation and allocation of financial resources** in accordance with organisational policies and legal requirements.

KNOWLEDGE REQUIREMENTS

You need to know and understand

Legal requirements

- legal requirements for the handling of information on the generation and allocation of financial resources

Monitoring and evaluation

- systems which may be used to review the generation and allocation of financial resources and their relative advantages and disadvantages to your area of work and available resources
- the information which is needed to review the generation and allocation of financial resources and how to collect this information
- how to select criteria which are appropriate to your organisation, its context and culture
- the commonly accepted performance measures for the generation and allocation of financial resources

- how to compare your organisation's performance with that of others
- alternative methods of generating and allocating financial resources which may be appropriate and how to evaluate these.

Organisational context

- the context and culture of the organisation and the implications of these for resource generation and allocation
- organisational requirements for the handling of information
- other organisations against which it is appropriate to compare your organisation's performance

Resource management

- the importance of continuously reviewing the generation and allocation of financial resources and your role and responsibilities in this regard.

EVIDENCE REQUIREMENTS

You must prove that you *review the generation and allocation of financial resources* to the National Standard of competence.

To do this, you must provide evidence to convince your assessor that you consistently meet **all** the performance criteria.

Your evidence must be the result of real work activities undertaken by yourself. Evidence from simulated activities is **not** acceptable for this element.

You must show evidence that you review at least **two** of the following methods for the **generation of financial resources**

- raising equity finance, obtaining loans, obtaining venture capital, negotiating with government for funds, obtaining sponsorship, creative and innovative approaches.

You must also show evidence that you review at least **one** of the following methods for the **allocation of financial resources**

- budgeted plans, internal bidding and departmental competition or collaboration, external bidding and interorganisational competition or collaboration.

You must, however, convince your assessor that you have the necessary knowledge, understanding and skills to be able to perform competently in respect of **all** types of **generation and allocation of financial resources** listed above.

Figure 4.12 MCI operational management Level 5, element B5.1 (Reproduced with permission of The Stationery Office)

Competency type	MANAGEMENT - BOARD DIRECTORS
BSC Ref	E2 / I3 / FC1
Strategic Competence Ref	S3 / S4 / S5 / S6
Competency area	MANAGING IN UNCERTAINTY (BD4)
Behavioural indicators	
Positive	**Negative**
Changing priorities are incorporated into work activities with minimal disruption to key deliverables	Change in priority is approached by presentation of obstacles and loss of efficiency and/or effectiveness
Top team and line reports are fully aware of and agree upon priorities for action	There is conflict amongst the top team with failure to co-operate for mutual benefit
A continual focus on results is maintained when managing priorities	An emphasis on process leads to misdirected efforts at managing priorities
Difficulties with achievement of priorities are discussed openly with a focus on solutions	Difficulties are not presented to the team at an early stage. Presentation is problem rather than solution-focused
Actively seeks ways to work more effectively with other members of the top team	Ignores conflicts, allowing them to be apparent to others
Enablers	**Hard Evidence**
Detailed understanding of the healthcare industry Impact of the external change on operations and future requirements Strategic thinking Results of prioritisation and change management Adaptability Innovation Staff motivational techniques Clear presentation and communication skills	Response to constant change which prioritises and achieves goals Feedback from top team and line reports Staff survey Achievement of objectives within timescales

Figure 4.13 An example of profiling with behavioural competencies

Profiling with behaviour competencies

Behavioural competencies can be used for profiling in a similar way, provided they are developed to be *measurable*. This type of competency is often presented in 'dimensions' and 'clusters', or with 'positive and negative' indicators, as shown in Figure 4.13. Just as 'units' in the outcome-based form of competences are used to profile roles, so the 'clusters/dimensions/competencies' in the behavioural style can be used.

Preparing a profile

Results of a profiling exercise can be incorporated into job descriptions, recruitment specs and appraisal documents or used for other HR functions, as illustrated in the next section.

This section has included examples of management competences/ies. Similar developments can (and should) be undertaken with other roles and job families to provide an integrated competence framework on which to 'hang' the HR functions.

4.6 REVISE THE HR FUNCTIONS

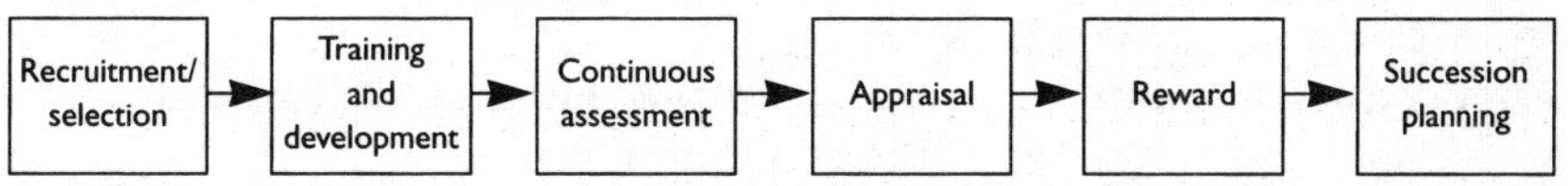

Figure 4.14 HR functions

Recruitment and Selection

Use competency profiles to prepare recruitment specifications and selection tools. Prepare selection exercises and interviews by focusing on activities and questions which will generate valid evidence of demonstrated competence.

Training and development

Use the detail within your competences/ies to design training and development activities that will help participants to acquire relevant skills and knowledge. Be creative with training and development options – use:

- formal training programmes
- on-the-job training
- coaching
- open programmes
- CBT
- distance learning
- discovery learning
- video and tape
- simulation
- skills tests.

Aim to establish a 'learning company' which Pedler (1991) defined as 'one which facilitates the learning of all its members and which continually transforms itself'.

The term 'Learning Organization' has been referenced by many writers. Garratt's work on top management development refers to directors as the 'business brain', with a hands-off approach. He also referred to 'double loop learning' of personal and organizational development (Garratt, 1988).

Peter Senge (1990) suggests four characteristics are needed for a learning organization:

- personal mastery (continuous improvement and development)
- shared vision (not top-down defined, but agreed)
- resonant mutual learning (team learning)
- fifth discipline (developing systems thinking).

There are many tools and techniques available to help with developing a culture of learning, continuous improvement and development. However, it is difficult to learn, train, develop and/or continuously improve unless everyone knows the expectations of performance in clear and measurable terms. This is where a competence framework provides a starting point for such development activities.

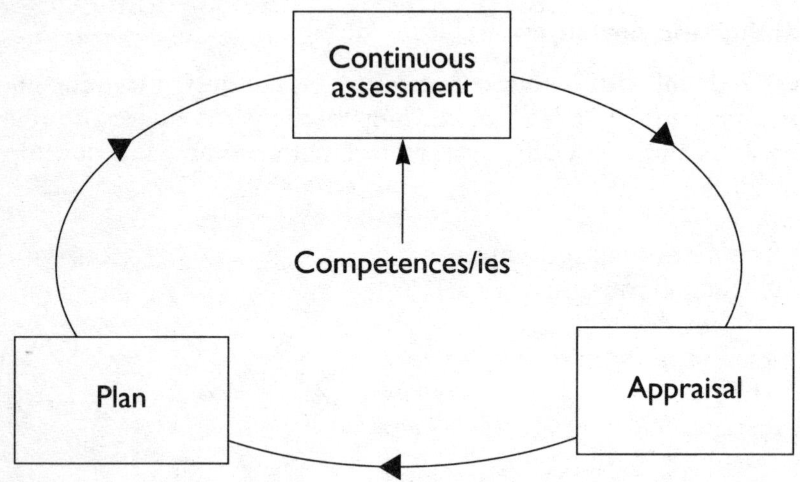

Figure 4.15 Using a competence framework for a continuous development cycle

Continuous assessment

Part of a manager's role is to continuously (day-to-day) assess people. To do this, managers need clear standards and assessment tools. These tools should be:

- user-friendly
- business-led
- valid
- motivational

Introducing NVQs (in the UK) is one way to provide assessment on a day-to-day basis. However, the 'bureaucratic' approach of hefty 'portfolios' should be avoided (see Fletcher, 1997b). Linking continuous assessment to training plans focuses individuals and managers on continuous improvement. Use of 'personal development records' or 'individual development plans' is becoming popular.

Appraisal

Appraisal is an opportunity to summarize continuous assessment, review performance, plan development and set new objectives. Too often the appraisal process is seen as a formal chore, completed, filed and forgotten.

If a competence framework is used to its full potential, appraisal focuses on review and planning as part of a continuous cycle; see Figure 4.16.

Reward and succession planning

Competency profiling provides a foundation for planning reward systems in a variety of ways. This includes linking to succession planning, as shown in Figure 4.16

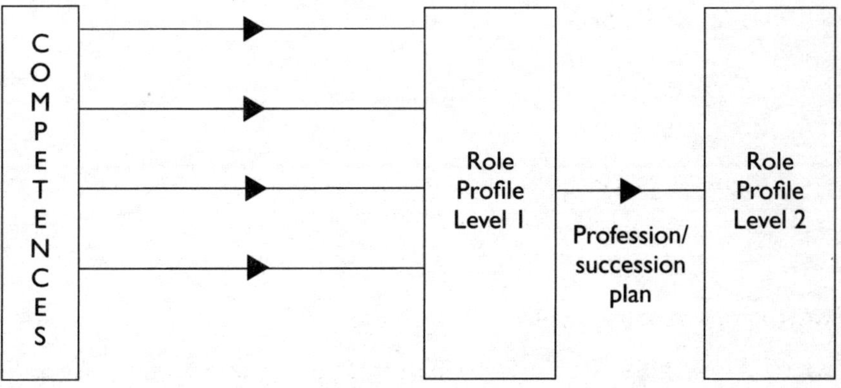

Figure 4.16 Profiling for reward and succession planning

Roles can be clearly differentiated in terms of competences/ies involved, and reward/succession (and development activities) planned accordingly (see MCL Group case study).

Many companies now use competence based-reward:
Blue Circle Cement (see *IRS Management Review*, 1996)
MCL Group (see case study, page 78)
Air UK (see case study, page 61)

Incentive and reward can be reviewed in a competence-based system with fewer grades, fewer job descriptions and more flexibility.

This section has given a broad overview of the use of a competence framework within the HR function. I hope it has met its objective of stimulating ideas for a fresh look at systems and processes.

References and Further Reading

Adair, J (1983) *Effective Leadership*, Gower, Aldershot.

Adair, J (1989) *Great Leaders*, Talbot Adair, Guildford.

Adair, J (1990) *Understanding Motivation*, Talbot Adair, Guildford.

Ansoff, H I (1984) *Implanting Strategic Management*, Prentice-Hall, New Jersey.

Ansoff, H I (1986) *Corporate Strategy*, Sidgwick and Jackson, London.

Ansoff, H I (1987) *Corporate Strategy*, Sidgwick and Jackson, London.

Belbin, R M (1981) *Management Teams – Why They Succeed or Fail*, Heinemann, Oxford.

Boulter N, Dalziel, M and Hill, J (1992) *People and Competencies*, Kogan Page, London.

Brown, A (1995) *Organisational Culture*, Pitman, London.

Campbell, A, Devine, M and Young, D (1990) *A Sense of Mission*, The Economist Books, London.

Campbell, A and Tawadey, K (1990) *Mission and Business Philosophy*, Heinemann, Oxford.

Campbell, A and Yeung, D (1991) 'Creating a Sense of Mission', *Long Range Planning*, 4, 4, 90–97.

Chandler, P (1962) *Strategy and Structure*, Harvard Business School Press, Boston.

Crosby, P B (1979) *Quality is Free*, McGraw-Hill, New York.

Deming, W E (1986) *Out of the Crisis*, Cambridge University Press, Cambridge.

Drucker, P F (1969) *The Age of Discontinuity*, Heinemann, Oxford.

Drucker, P F (1973) *Management: Tools, Responsibilities, Practices*, Heinemann, Oxford.

Drucker, P F (1992) *Managing for the Future*, Butterworth Heinemann, Oxford

Drucker, P F (1995) *The Practice of Management*, Harper & Row, New York.

Egan, G (1988) *Change Agent Skills*, University Associates, San Diego, California.

Fayol, H (1949) *General and Industrial Management* (trans. Constance Storrs), Pitman, London.

Fletcher, S (1993) *Integrating Quality and Competence*, Kogan Page, London.

Fletcher, S (1994) *NVQs; Standards and Competence: A Practical Guide for Managers and Trainers*, 2nd Edn, Kogan Page, London.

Fletcher, S (1997a) *Implementing your NVQ System*, Kogan Page, London.

Fletcher, S (1997b) *Competence Based Assessment Techniques*, 2nd Edn, Kogan Page, London.

Fletcher, S (1997c) *NVQ Assessment: A Handbook for the Paperless Portfolio*, Kogan Page, London.

Fletcher, S (1997d) *Analysing Competence: Tools and Techniques*, Kogan Page, London.

Fletcher, S (1997e) *Designing Competence Based Training*, 2nd Edn, Kogan Page, London.

Garratt, R (1988) *The Learning Organisation and the Need for Directors who Think*, Gower Publishing, Aldershot.

Hammer, M and Champy, J (1993) *Re-engineering the Corporation*, Nicholas Brealey Publishing, London.

Handy, C (1976) *Understanding Organisations*, Penguin, London.

Handy, C (1989) *The Age of Unreason*, Business Books, London.

Handy C, Gordon C, Gow, I and Randlescombe, C (1988) *Making Managers*, Pitman, London.

Harke, F (1995) *How to Re-engineer the Performance Management Process*, Kogan Page, London.

Harvey-Jones, J (1993) *Managing to Survive*, Heinemann, Oxford

Harvey-Jones, J (1988) *Making it Happen*, William Collins, Glasgow.

Hay/McBer (1992) *People and Competencies*, edited by Boulter, N, Dalziel, M and Hill, J, Kogan Page, London.

Herzberg, F (1968) 'One more time: How do you motivate employees?, *Harvard Business Review*, July.

Hofstede, G (1991) *Cultures and Organisations*, McGraw-Hill, Maidenhead.

Huczynski, A (1987) *Encyclopedia of Organisation Change Methods*,

Gower, Aldershot.

IRS Management Review (1996) October, 1:3.

IRS Management Review (1997) 'Cultural change', 1, 4.

Jaques, E (1976) *A General Theory of Bureaucracy*, Heinemann, Oxford.

Jessup, G (1991) *Outcomes: NVQs and the Emerging Model of Education and Training*, Falmer Press, London.

Juran, J R (1988) *Juran on Planning for Quality*, The Free Press, New York.

Kanter, R M (1984) *The Change Masters*, Simon and Schuster, New York.

Kanter, R M (1989) *When Giants Learn To Dance*, Simon and Schuster, New York.

Kaplan, R S and Norton, D P (1996) *The Balanced Scorecard: Translating strategy into action*, Harvard Business School Press, Boston.

Kennedy, C (1994) *Managing with the Guns*, Century, London.

Kepner, CH and Tregoe, B B (1981) *The New Rational Manager*, John Martin Publishing, London.

Kolb, D *et al.* (1984) *Organisational Psychology*, 4th edn, Prentice-Hall, Hemel Hempstead.

Kotter, J P (1990) *A Force for Change*, The Free Press, New York.

Kotter, J P and Hester, J L (1992) *Corporate Culture and Performance*, The Free Press, New York.

Lawler, E, Nadler, D and Minis, P (1983) *Organisational Change and the Conduct of Assessment Research in Assessing Organisational Change*, Wiley, Chichester.

Lynch, R and Cross, K (1995) *Measure Up! Yardsticks for continuous improvement*, Blackwell, Oxford.

McCormack, M (1984) *What They Don't Teach You at Harvard Business School*, William Collins, Glasgow.

McGregor, D (1960) *The Human Side of Enterprise*, McGraw-Hill, New York.

Mintzberg, H (1979) *The Structuring of Organisations*, Prentice-Hall, Englewood Cliffs, NJ.

Mintzberg, H (1980) *The Nature of Managerial Work*, 2nd edn, Harper & Row, New York.

Mintzberg, H (1989) *Mintzberg on Management*, Collier Macmillan, London.

Mintzberg, H (1994) *The Rise and Fall of Strategic Planning*, Prentice-Hall, Hemel Hempstead.

Moore, J I (1992) *Writers on Strategy and Strategic Management*, Penguin, Harmondsworth.

Ohmae, K (1983) *The Mind of the Strategist*, Penguin, Harmondsworth.

Ohmae, K (1990) *The Borderless World*, William Collins, Glasgow.

Ouchi, W (1981) *Theory Z*, Addison Wesley, New York.

Pascale, RB and Athos, AG (1986) *The Art of Japanese Management*, Penguin, Harmondsworth.

Pedler, M (1991) *The Learning Company: A strategy for sustainable development*, McGraw-Hill, Maidenhead.

Peters, T (1988) *Thriving on Chaos*, Macmillan, London.

Peters, T (1992) *Liberation Management*, Macmillan, London.

Peters, T and Waterman, R H Jr (1987) *In Search of Excellence*, Harper & Row, London.

Porter, M E (1980) *Competitive Strategy*, The Free Press, New York.

Porter, M E (1985) *Competitive Advantage*, The Free Press, New York.

Porter, M E (1990) *The Competitive Advantage of Nations*, Macmillan, London.

Pugh, D S (1990) *Organisation Theory – Selected Readings*, Penguin, Harmondsworth.

Revans, R W (1980) *Action Learning*, Blond and Briggs, London.

Royal Society of Arts (1995) *Tomorrow's Company: The role of business in a changing world*, RSA, London.

Sadler, P (1993) *Managing Talent*, The Economist Books, London.

Schein, E (1980) *Organisations and the Psychological Contract*, British Psychological Society, Leicester.

Schonberger, R J (1990) *Building a Chain of Customers*, The Free Press, New York.

Schwartz, P (1991) *The Art of the Long View*, Century, London.

Seashore, S (1983) (ed) *Issues in Assessing Organisational Change*, Wiley, Chichester.

Seashore, S *et al.* (1983) *Assessing Organisational Change*, Wiley, Chichester.

Senge, P (1990) *The Fifth Discipline – The art and practice of the learning organisation*, Doubleday, London.

Senge, P (1992) *The Fifth Discipline*, Century, London.

Senge, P (1994) *The Fifth Discipline Fieldbook*, Nicholas Brealy, London.

Stalk, G Jr and Hout, T M (1990) *Competing Against Time*, Collier Macmillan, London.

Stewart, J (1991) *Managing Change through Training and Development*, Kogan Page, London.

Swancheck and Campbell (1981) 'Competence/performance based

teacher education: the unfulfilled promise', *Education Technology* June, 5–10.

Taylor, F W (1947) *Scientific Management*, Harper & Row, New York.

Thomas, A B (1993) 'Twelve Organizational Principles', from *Company Organization Charts* by the American National Industrial Conference Board 1954, New York, reproduced in *Controversies in Management* (1993).

Waterman, R H Jr (1987) *The Renewal Factor*, Bantam, New York.

Waterman, R H Jr (1994) *The Frontiers of Excellence*, Nicholas Brealey, London.

Weber, M (1924) 'The Theory of Social and Economic Organisation', extract from *Organisation Theory* (ed. D S Pugh, 1990).

Wendt, H (1993) *Global Embrace*, HarperCollins, London.

Whitley, R C (1991) *The Customer Drive Company*, Business Books, London.

Index